1994

RACE, GENDER, and DESIRE

RACE, GENDER, and DESIRE

◆

*Narrative Strategies
in the Fiction of
Toni Cade Bambara,
Toni Morrison,
and Alice Walker*

ELLIOTT BUTLER-EVANS

TEMPLE UNIVERSITY PRESS

Philadelphia

Temple University Press, Philadelphia 19122
Copyright © 1989 by Temple University. All rights reserved
Published 1989
Printed in the United States of America

The paper used in this publication meets the minimum
requirements of American National Standard for Information
Sciences—Permanence of Paper for Printed Library Materials,
ANSI Z39.48-1984

Library of Congress Cataloging-in-Publication Data
Butler-Evans, Elliott, 1938–
Race, gender, and desire: narrative strategies in the fiction of
Toni Cade Bambara, Toni Morrison, and Alice Walker / Elliott Butler-
Evans.
p.   cm.
Bibliography: p. 211
Includes index.
ISBN 0-87722-608-3
1. American fiction—Afro-American authors—History and criticism.
2. American fiction—Women authors—History and criticism.
3. American fiction—20th century—History and criticism.
4. Bambara, Toni Cade—Political and social views.   5. Morrison,
Toni—Political and social views.   6. Walker, Alice, 1944-   —Political
and social views.   7. Race in literature.   8. Sex in
literature.   9. Politics and literature.   10. Semiotics and
literature.   I. Title.
PS374.N4B8   1989
813'.54'099287—dc 19   88-37887
CIP

Contents

◆

Acknowledgments

◆

The intensely intellectual and supportive setting of the Board of Studies in the History of Consciousness at the University of California at Santa Cruz is doubtlessly the primary enabling factor in my completion of this manuscript. I am particularly appreciative of the enthusiastic encouragement and support provided by Professors Hayden White, Donna Haraway, and Fredric Jameson. During my graduate studies, these scholars provided me with insights into some of the more recent developments in literary and cultural theory and encouraged me to apply them to my areas of interest.

Other members of the Santa Cruz community were also extremely helpful. Especially, I would like to thank Professor James Clifford, who introduced me to the area of cultural poetics, and Professor Helene Moglen, who significantly expanded my understanding of feminist literary theory. I am also extremely grateful to Ms. Billie Harris, administrative assistant in the History of Consciousness Board of Study, who provided strong moral support and practical advice to me during my tenure at the University.

Ongoing dialogues with colleagues have also been helpful in the production of this project. Among those always willing to offer constructive criticism were Vivek Dhareshwar, Nick Gravila, Jr., Harryette Mullen, Leslie Patrick-Stamp, Alvina Quintana, Garry Rolison, and Edward Stephenson. I found their comments and critiques extremely helpful in mapping out this study.

My colleagues in the English Department at the University of California at Santa Barbara were also helpful during the time I was completing this project. Professors Porter Abbott and Mark Rose, chairs of the department during this period, were always considerate in their scheduling of my courses and other responsibilities during this period. In the Center for Black Studies, Professor Cedric Robinson and Ms. Alyce Whitted consistently supported this project morally and intellectually, and generously gave of their energy and time during some rather difficult moments.

The special care and competence that Elinor Claire Flewellen brought to the initial editing of this manuscript was helpful during the period in which I made revisions; and Elizabeth Robinson's additional proofreading and editing were equally helpful in its completion.

This entire project is dedicated to my parents, the late Pearl Butler Evans and Louis Evans, who, through my formative years, were always strong sources of encouragement and inspiration.

RACE, GENDER, and DESIRE

Introduction

◆

DRAWING LARGELY on narratology, feminist cultural theory, semiotics, and Neo-Marxist concepts of ideology, this study explores the relationship between two conflicting discourses—one an inscription of race, the other focused on gender—within the fictional narratives of three Afro-American women writers. I argue that the fictive discourse of Toni Cade Bambara, Toni Morrison, and Alice Walker is often the site of dissonance, ruptures, and, particularly in each writer's more recent work, a kind of narrative violence generated by their articulations of these distinct and often contending expressions of desire.

While perhaps too rigidly implicated in Freudian discourse for my purposes, Peter Brooks's discussion of the relationship of desire to narrative provides a useful framework for an understanding of my project. Arguing that narratives "both tell of desire . . . and arouse and make use of desire as dynamic of signification," Brooks writes:

Desire is always there at the start of narrative, often in a state of initial arousal, often having reached a state of intensity such that movement must be created, action undertaken, change begun. . . . One could no doubt analyze the opening paragraph of most novels and emerge in each case with the image of desire taking on shape, beginning to seek its own object, beginning to develop a textual energetics.[1]

Elaborating on the role of desire in structuring narrative, Brooks examines the relationship of ambition to desire and the textual dynamics involved in "male plots of ambition."

Ambition is inherently totalizing, figuring the self's tendency to appropriation and aggrandizement, moving forward through the encompassment of more, striving to have, to do, and to be more. The ambitious hero thus stands as a figure of the reader's efforts to construct meanings in ever-larger wholes, to totalize his experience of human existence in time to grasp past, present, and future in a significant shape. (P. 38)

Readily acknowledging his blind spot to the "female plot," Brooks argues that

the female plot . . . takes a more complex stance towards ambition, the formation of an inner drive toward the assertion of selfhood in resistance to the overt and violating male plots of ambition, a counter-dynamic which, from the prototype of *Clarissa* on to *Jane Eyre* and *To the Lighthouse*, is only superficially passive, and in fact a reinterpretation of the vectors of plot. (P. 39)

While I would cautiously appropriate Brooks's formulations,[2] elements of both his plot models are related to my project. Certainly, the processes of "striving to have, to do, and to be more" are generally focuses of those narratives. Moreover, the "formation of an inner drive toward the assertion of selfhood" is usually a dominant theme in those works. Yet the material conditions under which these narratives are produced, the social and political contexts out of which they are generated, suggest narrative modes and inscriptions of desire more complex than those outlined by Brooks. The signifier "Black women writers," a product of these women's acts of naming and constructing themselves as well as others, denotes at least two modalities of difference and opposition. As I argue in Chapter Two, it encodes racial and gender questions. Often one finds in the authors' nonfiction writings strong statements of identification as Blacks, as women, or as both. The result is an attempted reconciliation of a fragmented self and a synthesis of racial and gender politics. This is the ideological enterprise that we observe in process in their narratives.

Inscribed in the works of Bambara, Morrison, and Walker are narrative strategies and the representation of a female subject somewhat similar to Catherine Belsey's theory of a "split subject" or "crisis in subjectivity."

In Lacanian theory entry into language is necessary to the child unless he or she is to become "sick"; at the same time entry into language inevitably creates a division between the subject of the enunciation and the subject of the enonce, the "I" who speaks and the "I" who is the subject of discourse. The subject is held in place in the discourse by the use of "I," but the "I" of this discourse is always a "stand-in" . . . a substitute for the "I" who speaks. It is this contradiction in the subject—between the conscious self, which is conscious in so far as it is able to feature in discourse, and the self which is only partially represented there—which constitutes the source of possible change.[3]

Belsey's critical orientation may be broadly described as Marxist–feminist. Citing examples from Donne, Wordsworth, and Shakespeare, she explains this division of the subject indicative of a historical period in which the mode of production is "radically threatened, or in transition, [and] confidence in the ideology of subjectivity is eroded" (p. 86). Departing somewhat from Belsey's generalized reading of the subject in contradiction, the argument I am advancing in terms of Bambara, Morrison, and Walker more closely resembles Julia Kristeva's concept of a "divided subject, even a pluralized subject, that occupies not a place of enunciation, but permutable, multiple, and mobile places."[4] I contend that both subject and narrative are fragmented as the works of these women become the locus of a struggle between the totalizing impulses of racial and gender political discourses, and that this struggle is a necessary development in generating the text's ideology.

Ideological Positions

The modes of inscribing these two discourses differ in these writers' works. Concern with the politics of race and gender is central to the narratives of Bambara, Morrison, and Walker;

however, the angles of focus and areas of emphases are generally determined and structured by the writer's specific ideological position. Because Morrison privileges the aesthetic in general and Afro-American mythology in particular, her insertion
of feminine desire becomes an extremely complex narrative
problem. Bambara's fiction, structured by a totalizing nationalist ideology, develops a feminist position within a generally
resisting social and cultural context. In constructing and asserting a "womanist" ideology, Walker's narratives (especially
her later works) are at the center of epistemological and narrative violence, engaged in confronting and challenging both
Black and white male readings of the world.

Each writer's ideological position might be said to determine the form and content of the narratives she produces. In
discussing these positions, however, I do not argue that authorial interpretation is the valid interpretive strategy by which
one might arrive at a univocal reading of the text. Dominick
LaCapra calls attention to the limitations inherent in such an
approach. Examining the relationship of the author's intentions to the text, and especially arguing against "assum[ing] a
proprietary relation between the author and the text as well as
a unitary meaning for utterance," he writes:

By presenting the text solely as "embodied" or realized "intention-
ality," [such a view] prevents one from formulating as an explicit
problem the question of relationship between intentions, insofar as
they can be plausibly reconstructed, and what the text may be argued to do or disclose. This relationship may involve multiple forms
of tension, including self-contestation. Not only may the intention
not fill out the text in a coherent or unified way; the intention or
intentions of the author may be uncertain or radically ambivalent.[5]

Such considerations are especially relevant in the works of
Bambara, Morrison, and Walker. The desire for synthesis, the
fusion of racial and gender politics, in their narratives is often
marked by tensions as one of the two discourses assumes privileged status. Hence, the attempt to achieve narrative closure

may leave ideological issues unresolved and open their works to multiple interpretations.

Finally, I should point out that in examining these writers' pretextual ideology, I am not committed to providing exhaustive, definitive statements. Instead, what I have attempted is to identify in each writer's nonfictional utterance key assertions related to race, gender, and desire. The problematizing of those ideological positions in specific narratives is the focal point of my study.

A recurrent theme in Toni Morrison's statements on Afro-American fiction is its relationship to the viability of Black culture. She argues that the loss of the Black oral tradition and the appropriation and incorporation of Black music by the dominant culture have necessitated the development and production of fictive discourse. Arguing for the significance of the novel, she writes:

For a long time, the art form that was healing for Black people was music. That music is no longer *exclusively* ours; we don't have exclusive rights to it. Other people sing it and play it; it is the mode of contemporary music everywhere. So another form has to take that place, and it seems to me that the novel is needed by African-Americans in a way that it was not needed before—and it is following along the lines of the function of novels everywhere. We don't live in places where we can hear those stories anymore; parents don't sit around and tell their children those classical, mythological archetypal stories that we heard years ago.[6]

In an earlier interview, Morrison addressed what she viewed as writing's potential as an instrument of empowerment. She argued that fiction, particularly the novel, provided the possibility of "becom[ing] coherent in the world" and that her novels should "clarify the roles that have become obscure [and] identify those things in the past that are useful and that are not."[7] Fictional narratives for Morrison, then, are part of a largely ethnographic enterprise. The semiotic construction of the race, through the inscription of the present and re-inscription of the past, becomes a mode of self-assertion in the world.

This raw material of the racial experience, according to Morrison, should also be shaped by a consciousness of form. Arguing that the novel should be "beautiful and powerful," she emphasizes the importance of technique, particularly its relationship to the act of enabling the reader to participate with the writer in the construction of the work. Commenting on Black cultural practices that she incorporates in her works, Morrison writes:

One of [the major characteristics of Black art] is the ability to be both print and oral literature; to combine those two aspects so that the stories can be read in silence, of course, but one should be able to hear them as well. It should try deliberately to make you stand up and make you feel something profoundly in the same way that a Black preacher requires his congregation to speak, to join him in the sermon, to behave in a certain way, to stand up and to weep and to cry and to accede or to change and to modify—to expand on the sermon that is being delivered. In the same way that musician's music is enhanced when there is a response from the audience. Now in a book, which closes, after all . . . to try to make that happen also.[8]

This foregrounding of Afro-American culture and what I later identify as the aesthetic ideology in Morrison's narratives problematize the representational status of the female subject. Not only is that status problematized by the ideology of the text, but also a pretextual ideology in which Morrison explores issues related to women's writing and feminist discourse in general. In an interview with Claudia Tate, Morrison addresses differences in writing strategies that characterize the works of Black women, Black men and white men, and white women. Asserting that "Black men don't write very differently from white men," she emphasizes the "enormous difference" in the narratives of Black and white women:

Aggression is not new to black women as it is to white women. Black women seem able to combine the nest and the adventure. They don't see conflicts in certain areas as do white women. They are both safe harbor and ship; they are both inn and trail. We, black women, do both. We don't find these places, these roles, mutually exclusive. . . .

There's a male/female thing that's also different in the works of black and white women writers, and this is good. There's a special kind of domestic perception that has its own violence in the writings by black women—not bloody violence, but violence nonetheless. Love in the Western notion is full of possession, distortion, and corruption. It's a slaughter without the blood.[9]

This assertion of difference is concomitant with Morrison's distancing herself from a largely white feminist movement that she views as irrelevant to the special historical conditions of Black women.[10] This distancing is also implied in Morrison's rejection of feminist theory in general. Responding to Mari Evans's query about "the necessity to develop a specific Black feminist model of critical inquiry," Morrison states:

I don't have much to say about that . . . except that I think there is more danger in it than fruit, because any model of criticism or evaluation that excludes males from it is as hampered as any model of criticism of Black literature that excludes women from it. For critics, models have some function. They like to talk in terms of models and developments and so on, so maybe it's of some use to them, but I suggest that even for them there is some danger in it.[11]

The ideological context in which Morrison's fiction is created, then, is one that valorizes and foregrounds a sense of Black community, or to use her terms, "village" or "tribe." This is reinforced by the writer's opposition to feminist discourse in general. In Chapter Three I consider the manner in which these priorities constitute containment strategies that suppress feminine desire in Morrison's fiction.

Toni Cade Bambara's fiction is largely overdetermined by an ideological position in which writings by Blacks are necessarily oppositional. As a self-described nationalist–feminist–socialist, she views her works as discourse in opposition to two modes of domination: racism, which, she argues, allows whites to define and determine the existences of Blacks; and patriarchal oppression, through which all males exercise hegemonic privileges in their relationship with women.

For Bambara, the struggle against racism is embodied in a battle for "truth," a truth that stands in opposition to the interpretation and representation of Blacks in the discourses of whites. Like other artists in the largely male Black Aesthetic movement, she argues that the writer has a responsibility to deconstruct the White/Black binary opposition that underpins dominant discourse and generates "revolutionary" paradigms of representations and values. In an interview with Claudia Tate, she elucidated this position:

I start with the recognition that we are at war, and that war is not simply a hot debate between the capitalist camp and the socialist camp over which economic/political/social arrangement will have hegemony in the world. It's not just the battle over turf and who has the right to utilize resources for whomsoever's benefit. The war is also being fought over the truth: what is the truth about human nature, about the human potential? My responsibility to myself, my neighbors, my family and the human family is to try to tell the truth. That ain't easy. There are so few truth-speaking traditions in this society in which the myth of "Western civilization" has claimed the allegiance of so many. We have rarely been encouraged and equipped to appreciate the fact that truth works, that it releases the Spirit and that it is a joyous thing.[12]

In the interview–essay that appears in Mari Evans's collection, Bambara further develops her position:

What informs my work as I read it . . . are the basic givens from which I proceed. One, we are at war. Two, the natural response to oppression, ignorance, evil, and mystification is wide-awake resistance. Three, the natural response to stress and crisis is not breakdown and capitulation, but transformation and renewal too. The question I raise [in all of my works] is, is it natural (sane, healthy, wholesome, in our interest) to violate the contracts/covenants we have with our ancestors, each other, our children, our selves, and God.[13]

The battle for "truth" that Bambara would wage against racism is echoed in her struggle against sexism. In her edited collection of Black feminist essays, the first publication of its kind, she argued that central to those discourses empowered to describe and define reality—psychology, the natural sciences, literature—were research strategies that perpetuated the subjugation of Black women. Addressing this male construction of an empowering discourse and its attendant oppression of Black women, she observed:

When the experts (white or Black, male) turn their attention to the Black woman, the reports get murky, for they usually clump the men and women together and focus so heavily on what white people have done to the psyches of Blacks, that what Blacks have done to and for themselves is overlooked, and what distinguishes the men from the women forgotten.[14]

Revolutionary consciousness for Bambara, then, involves a struggle against racism (oppression from external forces) and sexism (generated by both external and internal forces). She advocates a radical restructuring of male–female relationships, proposing the rejection of masculine and feminine roles and the construction of a Selfhood/Blackhood that displaces gender differentiation, thereby enabling the "Black community" to move in unison against racist oppression. With this objective in mind, she writes:

I have always opposed the stereotypic definitions of "masculine" and "feminine" because I always found that either/or implicit in those definitions antithetical to what I was all about and what revolution for self is all about. I am beginning to see . . . the usual notions of sexual differentiation in roles as obstacles to political consciousness, that the way those terms are generally defined and acted upon in this part of the world is a hindrance to development.[15]

Toni Cade Bambara's fiction, therefore, involves a complex rewriting of Black nationalist discourse. The desire of

the female subject, largely omitted or marginalized in that discourse, is not only radically inscribed but foregrounded. In this
project I focus on the manner in which that desire surfaces in
the first collection of short stories, is more directly but ambivalently textualized in the second volume, and erupts violently
in *The Salt Eaters.*

Four definitions of *womanist* serve as epigraphs to *In Search of
Our Mothers' Gardens,* a collection of essays written by Alice
Walker over twenty-six years and culled from a number of jour-
nals, periodicals, and books. The first definition locates the
term within the context of "black folk expression of mother to
female children" and establishes it as a sign of a "black feminist or feminist of color." The second identifies the term with
a woman

who loves other women sexually and/or nonsexually. Appreciates
and prefers women's culture, women's emotional flexibility . . . and
women's strength. Sometimes loves individual men sexually and/or
nonsexually. Committed to survival and wholeness of entire people,
male and female. Not a separatist, except periodically for health.
Traditionally a universalist.

The third definition celebrates the sensuality and spirituality
of the womanist as one who loves "music, dance, the Spirit,
love and food and roundness, struggle, the Folk, herself. Regardless." The final definition is phrased in form of an analogy:
"Womanist is to feminist as purple is to lavender." [16]
    These definitions provide a framework for interpreting the
essays that comprise the volume and an indication of an ideological position in progress. The movement from the specific
racial reference in the first definition to a broader application
of the term in the second definition and the somewhat open
definition of the term in the last definition: "Womanist is to
feminist as purple is to lavender." [17]
    Walker's fiction, then, can be said to be structured by a
complex ideological position that oscillates between her iden-

tity as "Black feminist" or "woman-of-color" and a generalized feminist position in which race is subordinated. Her primary emphasis, however, is consciousness of herself as a Black woman empowered to narrate the stories of Black women who are past or present creators of a Black female culture. Her role, then, is one of enabling Black women, especially those most marginalized by race, caste, and class, to have their voices heard and their histories read.

Walker argues that this focusing on the inner world of Blacks has broad political implications. In a discussion with Claudia Tate on the preeminence of "intimate male–female encounters" over social confrontations in the narratives of Black women, Walker comments:

> Twentieth century black women writers all seem to be much more interested in the black community, in intimate relationships, with the white world as a *backdrop*. . . . There just has not been enough examination or enough application of findings to real problems in our day-to-day living. Black women continue to talk about intimate relations so that we can recognize what is happening when we see it, then maybe there will be some change in behavior on the part of men *and* women.[18] (Emphasis in original)

This position is strongly reinforced by the respect Walker expresses for Jean Toomer's works and her reverence for Zora Neale Hurston as a writer whose works Walker views as embodying "racial health; a sense of black people as complex, complete *undiminished* human beings, a sense that is lacking in so much black writing and literature" (*Search*, 85). The representations of Black life and culture in her works, however, are strongly motivated by the belief that "the truth about any subject only comes when all the sides of the story are put together, and their different meanings make one new one" (*Search*, 49).

Telling the "truth" involves what Walker identifies as "writing the missing parts to the other writer's story." Within Black narratives these gaps or omissions are largely signified by what she identifies as general unauthentic representations of Black women. Addressing this issue of marginalization of women, she writes:

The absence of models in literature as in life, to say nothing of painting, is an occupational hazard for the artist, simply because models in art, in behavior, in growth of spirit and intellect—even if rejected—enrich and enlarge one's view of existence. Deadlier still, to the artist who lacks models, is the curse of ridicule, the bringing to bear on an artist's best work, especially his or her most original, most strikingly deviant, only a fund of ignorance and the presumption that, as an artist's critic, one's judgment is free of restrictions imposed by prejudice and is well-informed, indeed, about all the art in the world that really matters. (*Search*, 4–5)

This general sketch of the pretextual ideological framework of Walker's fiction will be developed in my discussions of individual works; here my intention is to identify the concerns that inform that framework and structure her novels. What is at stake is the fictional inscription of two modes of historical discourse. A commitment to write the "authentic" lives of "real" Black people occupies textual space with an urgency to tell the specific stories of Black women. The contentious relationship inherent in that enterprise shapes my reading of Walker.

The Concepts of Ideology, Feminine, and Feminist

In an effort to clarify a significant aspect of my critical approach in this project, I should point out that my use of *ideology* is identified with two aspects related to the narratives under examination. We might turn to Raymond Williams, who addresses some of the issues generated by discussions of ideology within Marxist literary theory, and which, in my opinion, would be related to any critical enterprise that focused on ideology and cultural practice. Williams identifies three understandings of ideology.

1. A system of beliefs characteristic of a particular class or group

2. A system of illusory beliefs—false ideas or false consciousness —which can be contrasted with true or scientific knowledge

3. The general process of the production of meanings and ideas [19]

The first and third definitions suggest my concerns. Having identified the pretextual ideologies of the three writers—their personal statements on race, gender, and the fictional pro- duction—I turn to the manner in which specific strategies of narration and representation produce a specific textual ideol- ogy. In applying William's third definition, I adapt Althusser's concept of ideology as "represent[ing] the imaginary relation- ship of individuals to their real conditions of existence." [20] For this study, the Althusserian concept must be revised because the literature I examine is that of a subhegemonic group; Thus, the emphasis on ideology's role in reproducing the conditions of production is largely irrelevant here. What is significant in these narratives is the manner in which specific textual strate- gies construct a Black female subject torn by allegiances to race and gender politics and engaged in acts of self-assertion and affirmation. The ideological issues generated by these narra- tives are produced by what Williams would generally designate as an emergent cultural formation, that is, one in which "new meanings and values, new practices, new significances and experiences are continually being created." [21]

Just as working with the concept of ideology involved seri- ous revising and rethinking of the concept, my elaboration of *feminine* and *feminist* presented significant challenges. Annette Kuhn has explored some of the complexities involved in the application of the terms to film, focusing on author, text, and reception, [22] but the historian Linda Gordon's understanding of these terms, her observation of "an inescapable tension" be- tween female and feminist consciousness, supports the frame- work of my analysis. Gordon writes:

Throughout various parts of feminist scholarship today . . . there is an attempt to reach a false resolution of [that] tension . . . a reso- lution that would obliterate the distinction between the female and the feminist. It seems to me important to claim both. The female is ourselves, our bodies and our socially constructed experience. It is not the same as feminism, which is not a "natural" exertion of that experience but a controversial political interpretation and struggle, by no means universal to women [23]

Gordon's distinctions generally structure my interpretations of the works of Bambara, Walker, and Morrison. I have taken care to distinguish between the somewhat implicit feminist articulations in works such as Bambara's early short stories and the explicit statements in Walker's later novels. At moments I have designated an episode "feminine/feminist" to call attention to complex modes of textualization in specific narratives in which the concepts overlap somewhat.

Finally, I must address issues related to my involvement in the materials I examine in this effort. My participation in several seminars in the History of Consciousness program at the University of California at Santa Cruz during the academic years 1983 and 1984 introduced me to fresh insights into poststructuralist cultural theory in general and feminist theory, narratology, and semiotics in particular. As a Black male, I was interested in the possible applications of theoretical insights to aspects of Afro-American culture. Particularly I was interested in the relationship of processes of narration to issues of self-construction and empowerment. The pioneering work of Houston Baker and Henry Louis Gates arguably suggested new directions in Afro-American criticism. Yet both scholars, it would seem, stressed racial discourse and generally downplayed the ideological issues generated by the representation of Black women in the narratives of Black males and the strategies of self-representation that characterized the writings of Black women. Moreover, much of the critical examination of Black women writers by other scholars focused on the regeneration of neglected texts and the establishment of a canon. What was generally missing were attempts to examine the application of theory to the texts of Black women writers. My study initially addressed that void.

It is not my intention to produce singular, univocal readings of the narratives I have selected, asserting some irrevocable and final bodies of meanings. Instead, to use a somewhat abused term, I am seeking to read "deconstructively," that is, to explore margins and centers of individual narratives to locate their moments of tension (and sometimes gaps and omissions) and to illuminate the significance involved in these in the production of ideology. The reading approach I employ resonates with Fredric Jameson's advice to critics:

In matter of art, and particularly of artistic perception . . . it is wrong to want to decide, to want to resolve a difficulty: what is wanted is a kind of mental procedure which suddenly shifts gears, which throws everything in an inextricable tangle one floor higher, and turns the very problem itself . . . into its own solution by widening its frame in such a way that it now takes its own mental processes as well as the object of those processes.[24]

In this study, I am primarily concerned with what I choose to call the politics of narration. While this text might be considered by some readers insufficiently assertive or too "objective" to be received as feminist criticism, it attempts to address the issue of narrative fragmentation in the writings of three Afro-American women in the context of pretextual ideologies and material conditions that are likely to overdetermine texts that are race and gender specific. It is not my intention to discredit or undermine traditional approaches to Afro-American women's fiction. My endeavor might best be read as an intervention through which contemporary theoretical discourse is opened to a new object of study, and the production of ideology in the writings of Afro-American women is illuminated through the uses of new interpretive strategies.

ONE

◆

Producing the Signs of Race:
Self-Fashioning in
Black Aesthetic Discourse

In the fiction of Morrison, Walker, and Bambara, as in the works of Black women writers in general, the construction of race-specific narratives that highlight a gendered subject has required the fusion of two discourses. The representation of race requires its own semiotic strategies, featuring ethnic differences and developing coherent patterns of self-construction. Conversely, because racial discourse, particularly when it stresses opposition, gravitates toward totality, threatening to erase all nuances, it often conflicts with the construction of a female character. Hence, in their attempts to construct and narrate an identity, Black women writers pursue a strategy that attempts to resolve tensions between the two discourses.

In this chapter I examine the racial discourse that influences Black writers, both men and women. Such discourse is strongly grounded in modes of representation that primarily drew upon sign-production strategies that contributed to Black nationalist ideology. Within and against this discourse, Morrison, Walker, and Bambara have produced their fiction.

The Black Aesthetic Movement

In the mid 1960s, narratives emerged that significantly affected the production, reception, and criticism of Afro-American literature for nearly a decade. Under the broad rubric of the Black Aesthetic, these texts focused on the semiotic mediations of Black "reality" by Black artists and critics, challenged and deconstructed received definitions of literature, and, perhaps above all, were in opposition to the dominant literature. Central to their enterprise were three objectives:

1. Through elaborate self-representation, architects of the Black Aesthetic movement attempted to produce a counter-discourse, generally identified as Black consciousness, to displace the dominant Western mode of representing Black "reality."

2. Through semiotic mediation, particularly the appropriation of the experiences that undergirded ordinary Black life, they attempted to construct narratives of a mythical Black nation.

3. Seeking to deconstruct the art–politics opposition, they challenged "literary" texts, particularly the novel, and argued for the development of cultural forms that more readily lent themselves to oral production, such as poetry and one-act plays.

The political significance of Black Aesthetic discourse has been very ably addressed by Houston Baker. Locating numerous texts that constituted the discourse in their specific historical context, he viewed them as a "direct counterthrust by an emergent generation to an integrationist Poetics' call for a general, raceless, and classless community of men and women in America." Examining the writings of several Black Aestheticians, largely Larry Neal, Amiri Baraka, and Stephen Henderson, and using Thomas Kuhn's concept of a "paradigm shift," Baker saw the Black Aesthetic movement as a nationalist movement driven by a romantic world view and a largely Marxist political perspective.[1]

A closer examination of some of these issues illuminates Black Aesthetic discourse as a specific mode of cultural practice structured by the semiotic construction of race or ethnicity. Particularly its grounding in what Eco has called "semiotic guerrilla warfare" mark it as oppositional discourse characterized by self-representation. Black Aestheticians attempted to represent Black life as lived by the Black masses, to fashion identities that corresponded with those of ordinary Black people, and to displace Western cultural hegemony. Raymond Williams's concepts of ideology as "a system of beliefs characteristic of a particular class or group" and "the general process of the production of meanings and ideas" characterize the ideological process of Black Aesthetic discourse. The construction of a particular class or group, in this case the "Black nation," is the product of semiosis, depending on semiotic representations of certain aspects of Black "life styles," and these individual signs coalesce to form the semiotic infrastructure of Black Aesthetic ideology.

An Emergent Cultural Nationalism

The development of an ideology arguably depends on the existence of enabling material conditions—similar to Bakhtin's concept of an "ideological environment." Employing the phrase to denote various social practices that enter into human consciousness and relate to its activities (e.g., cultural production), he writes:

Social man is surrounded by ideological phenomena, by object-signs of various types and categories: by words in their multifarious forms of their realizations . . . by scientific statements, religious symbols and beliefs, works of art and so on. All of these things in their totality comprise the ideological environment, which forms a solid ring around man. And man's consciousness lives and develops in this environment. Human consciousness [comes into existence] through the medium of the surrounding world.[2]

The ideological environment in which Black Aesthetic discourse emerged was one in which other race-specific texts of the period were marked by a single priority: the social and political empowerment of Black Americans. The doctrine of Black Power, arguably the master text, forcefully addressed this issue. Charles Hamilton, co-author with Stokely Carmichael

of *Black Power: The Politics of Liberation,* read the violent eruptions in the ghettoes as narratives of political desire. He rejected descriptions of those events as "riots" and argued that
they constituted an oppressed minority's answer to a structure
of domination:

> The revolts are overt denials of legitimacy. True they are threatening
> "law and order"—not to get a color television set, but to say that a
> wholly new norm of "law and order" must be established. . . . [They
> are] revolts against the anachronistic principles of legitimacy. They
> are revolts that say in no uncertain terms that Black people no longer
> believe in this system.[3]

Narratives of urban unrest and civil disorder revealed political desire and paralleled similar texts of social change during
the period. They were represented in a semiotics of fashion
(e.g., the appropriation and modification of African modes of
dress as signs of nationalist identity; linguistic resistance to cultural domination, marked by the displacement of "standard"
English, viewed as the language of whites and the bourgeoisie
in general, and a stress on "Black English"; and the rewriting and reinvention of Christian liturgy, in which traditional
religious symbolism was displaced by radical signs from Black
culture).[4]

These developments were perhaps most clearly analyzed by
Alvin Pouissant, a Harvard University psychiatrist who has
written extensively on Afro-American culture. Pouissant argued that the failure of integrationist ideology adequately to
address Black Americans' self-concept created a need for them
to turn inward, to their own community, for self-esteem. Ex-
plaining the psychological benefits of the emerging cultural
nationalism, he wrote: "Unfortunately, the white man cannot
give Negroes black consciousness. Negro Americans must give
it to each other. . . . [Black people] must undo the centuries
of brainwashing by the white man and substitute in its stead a
positive self-image and positive concept of oneself."[5]

The Black Aesthetic movement, then, was materially aided

by an ideological environment marked by penetrating texts of Black self-construction. These heterogeneous verbal and non-verbal narratives had a single thrust: the construction of a racial identity. The process was somewhat akin to that outlined by Irene Portis Winner in her adaptation of Lotman's textual modalities to theorize a semiotics of ethnicity.[6] Black Aesthetic discourse established boundaries marked by oppositions: inner world/outer world, Black/white, we/they, oppressed/oppressor. Out of this strategy of narrating "the Black experience" emerged a unique mode of self-imaging that produced Black identities different from, and in conflict with, the dominant culture. This self-fashioning was later to be called "Black consciousness."

The Politics of Self-Fashioning

Stephen Greenblatt's work in cultural poetics provides an effective theoretical tool for the examination of the modes of self-construction that characterized Black Aesthetic narratives, although it focuses on texts essentially different from those under consideration here. Central to Greenblatt's theory is the concept of "self-fashioning," a term he uses to denote "a distinctive personality, a characteristic address to the world, a consistent mode of perceiving and behaving." This mode of encountering the world places its emphasis on the construction of a self that is different from, and removed from, a hostile Other. Greenblatt writes:

Self-fashioning derives its interest precisely from the fact that it functions without a sharp regard for literature and social life. It invariably crosses the boundaries between the creation of literary characters, the shaping of one's own identity, the experience of being molded by forces outside one's control, the attempt to fashion other selves.[7]

The relevance of self-fashioning to the production of Black Aesthetic narratives can be stated without question. The self-imaging of Black Aestheticians was largely generated by their construction of whites as "alien and hostile Others," "produced almost exclusively in language," and consisted of displacement of the authority invested in Western epistemology by an oppositional Black consciousness. In order to understand the semiotic history undergirding this enterprise, however, we must turn to an earlier text: Richard Wright's "Blueprint for Negro Literature."

Written and published in 1937, when Wright was a young member of the Communist party, the "Blueprint" reproduced in a literary treatise Lenin's position on "The Negro Question." In an attempt to increase its sparse Black membership, the Sixth World Congress of the Communist International in 1935 proposed a Black republic in America in the South Atlantic states. This proposal became part of its platform in 1936. Indifference or hostility to the proposal from Black leaders forced abandonment of the project, but Wright, at the time a strong apologist for the party, incorporated in his "Blueprint" the concept of a Black nation.

Wright's representation of Black life, determined largely by his political ideology, provided him with the means to distance himself from writers of the Black middle class. Invoking Lenin, Wright asserted that Black writers generally represented the "petty bourgeois section of an 'oppressed minority,' " that their sole interest was to emulate and reflect the values of the white middle class in an attempt to "lift themselves into a higher social sphere." His characterization of their writing was particularly devastating. He argued that

Negro writing in the past has been confined to humble novels, poems, and plays, prim and decorous ambassadors who went a begging to white America. They entered the court of White American Public Opinion dressed in knee-pants of servility, curtsying to show that the negro was not inferior, that he was human, and that he had a life comparable to that of other people.[8]

In opposition to representations advanced by these writers, Wright posited an alternative construction of Black "reality."

His approach was to map out a semiotic strategy that would capture the "nationalist aspects" of Black life, which he viewed as having three components: the social institutions engendered by racial discrimination and segregation; the oral practices characterized in folklore, spirituals, and blues; and the overall life styles of the Black peasantry and working classes.

This perception of the viability and political potential of Black life structured Wright's concept of the Black nation. For him, these elements signified that which differentiated Black culture from the dominant culture and established its oppositional character:

Blues, spirituals, and folktales [he wrote] recounted from mouth to mouth; the whispered words of a Black mother to her Black daughter of the ways of men; the confidential wisdom of a Black father to his Black son; the swapping of sex experiences on street corners from boy to boy in the deepest vernacular; work songs sung under the blazing suns—all these form the channel through which racial wisdom followed. (P. 40)

Central to Wright's construction of Black culture was his reading of it as a signifier of repressed political consciousness. Connecting folklore with political desire, he wrote:

The negro has a folklore which embodies the memories and hopes of his struggle for freedom. Not yet caught in paint or stone, and as yet but feebly depicted in the poem and the novel, the negroes' most powerful images of hope and despair still remain in the fluid state of daily speech.

Here are those vital beginnings of a recognition of value in life as it is lived, a recognition that marks the emergence of a new culture in the shell of the old. And at the moment this process starts, at the moment when a people begins to realize a meaning in their suffering, the civilization that engendered that suffering is doomed. (P. 41)

The interpretation of folklore as a signifier of repressed political desire led Wright to posit a specific role for the Black artist and, even more important, linked Wright with the later Black Aesthetic movement. His emphasis on the repressed political content of folklore, particularly his suggestion that the body of signs constituting its form might be reconstructed as a larger myth of Black identity, was the earliest expression of the Black Aesthetic movement. The writer's responsibility, as Wright envisioned it, was primarily one of semiotically reconstructing and narrating Black "reality." He argued that the writer's task was to create "myth and symbols that inspire faith in life" and in so doing "[mold] the lives and consciousness of the masses towards new goals rather than [continue] to beg the question of the Negro's humanity."

The semiotic enterprise undertaken by Wright in his "Blueprint," then, was motivated by a specific political agenda. Central to Wright's argument was the necessity for readers to embrace a "Marxist conception of reality." They would experience their lived experiences, or conditions, as reproduced in the literary text, and in doing so, would be moved to a higher level of consciousness. Literature produced by Afro-Americans would allow readers to understand "the relationship between a Negro woman hoeing cotton in the Southland to the men who loll in swivel chairs in Wall Street and take the fruits of her toils" (p. 44).

Symbolic Inversion

The Black Aesthetic discourse of the 1960s, while implicated in semiotic constructions of Black life similar to those advanced by Wright, placed a stronger emphasis on symbolic inversion. This process has been defined as "any act of expressive behavior which inverts, contradicts, abrogates, or in some fashion presents an alternative to commonly held cultural codes, values, and norms be they linguistic, literary or artistic, religious, or social and political."[9] The major thrust of Black Aesthetic narratives as oppositional or alternative texts was the production of alternative representations of Black life, positing significant self-reconstruction and definition, and the deconstruction of the ideological assumptions underpinning

Western constructions of reality. The slogan "Black is beautiful" evokes Bakhtin's view of ideological conflict as essentially a struggle over the sign in which "any current curse word can become a word of praise, any current truth must inevitably sound to many other people as the greatest lie." [10]

In their strategies of symbolic inversion, the authors of Black Aesthetic texts emphasized the relationship of their narratives to other discourses that constituted the ideological environment. Hoyt Fuller, a major figure in the Black Aesthetic movement, linked emerging Black consciousness in politics to similar developments in art in general and literature in particular. Fuller argued:

Just as Black intellectuals have rejected the NAACP, on the one hand, the other two major political parties, on the other, and gone off in search of new and more effective means and methods of seizing power, so revolutionary Black writers have turned their back on the old "certainties" and struck out in new, if uncharted directions. They have begun a journey toward a Black Aesthetic. [11]

Difference, opposition, and change are key elements in the formation of Black Aesthetic discourse, whose theorists were challenged to illuminate the Western, or white, aesthetic to which they were opposed. Addison Gayle, another major figure of the movement, saw Western aesthetics as transhistorical cultural hegemonic practices implicated in both the cultural and political oppression of Blacks. He argued for a displacement of that discourse of racism:

The distinction between whiteness as beautiful (good) and blackness as ugly (evil) appears very early in the literature of the Middle Ages —in the Morality Plays of England. Heavily influenced by Platonism and Christianity, these plays set forth the distinctions which exist today. To be white was to be pure, good, universal, and beautiful; to be black was to be impure, evil, parochial, and ugly. [12]

Thus one of the major objectives of the Black Aesthetic was the dismantling of Western modes of symbolic domination: the privileged position of white "reality," the inscription in Western narratives of Blacks as deficient and lacking in one quality or another, and strategies of representation and narration that influenced the West's reading of white culture as the socially sanctioned epistemological position to which all should subscribe. The struggle is succinctly argued by Larry Neal:

The motive behind the Black Aesthetic is the destruction of the white thing, the destruction of white ideas, and white ways of looking at the world. The new aesthetic is mostly predicated on ethics which ask the question: whose vision of the world is finally more meaningful, ours or the white oppressors? What is truth? Or more precisely, whose truth shall we express, that of the oppressed or of the oppressors.[13]

It was, therefore, not solely its opposition to Western representations and cultural production in general that structured Black Aesthetic discourse. A necessary concomitant to this challenging, displacement, and desired destruction of the White Aesthetic was the construction of a Black reality marked by difference. The project became one of constructing new definitions of Blackness, creating narratives that would serve as counterdiscourses to hegemonic narratives, and generating alternative paradigms of representations of Black life.

One strategy involved in this "corrective" narration of Black American life consisted of situating the Black American struggle within an international context. Aided by liberation movements in Africa, as well as the Vietnam crisis, Black Aestheticians encoded the insurrection in America's urban areas as small units of a larger struggle against Western imperialism. Linking this reading of the political situation directly with developments in the artistic realm, Larry Neal spoke of the Black Aesthetic as encompassing "most of the usable elements of Third World Culture" (P. 30) and saw Black Americans and Third World people united in a common struggle.

Locating the Black American experience within an international context provided Black Aesthetic discourse with a semantic frame of reference through which a body of signs could be generated. The dominant culture was constructed under the sign of "The Mother Country"; although geographically diverse and culturally heterogeneous, Black communities in general were textually inscribed as the "colonies"; and the masses of people who made up those communities were constructed as the "nation" of oppressed Blacks.[14]

"The artist and political activist are one"

The emphasis on nationalism in Black Aesthetic discourse, of course, signaled a significant departure from Wright's concept. While Wright's semiotic construction of a Black nation was implicitly involved in the mirroring of an anterior reality that would lead readers to a "higher" truth, Black Aestheticians saw the realization of the Black nation as the truth to be reached and to become a source for self-fashioning and empowerment. Particularly in Black Aestheticians' position on the unimportance of the written text, especially the novel, is this most clearly evident.

In Wright's "Blueprint," as I have suggested, he spoke to the cultural richness of a Black subculture grounded in oral and nonverbal practices. For him, however, that culture simply informs the semiotic infrastructure of Black cultural production. The primacy of the literary text—to the extent that folk culture is something to be *transcended*—is consistently in the foreground in Wright's treatise. Black Aestheticians, conversely, deemphasized the literary text, designating it as bourgeois art removed from "the people." Larry Neal forcefully addressed this issue:

We can learn more about what poetry is by listening to the cadences in Malcolm [X]'s speeches than from most Western poetics. Listen to James Brown scream. Ask yourself, then: Have you ever heard a Negro poet sing like that? Of course not, because we have been tied to the texts, like most white poets. The text could be destroyed, and no one would be hurt in the least by it. The key is in the music. Our music has always been ahead of our literature, except for, perhaps, the folktale.[15]

In addition to informing the ideological position of Black Aesthetic discourse, this reassessment of literature served two other purposes. It created a context in which cultural forms such as poetry, folklore, and one-act plays were highly valued because of their direct relationship to oral modes of cultural production. More important, however, echoing Wright's earlier pronouncements, it advanced the attack on the class status and political loyalties of traditional Black writers, identifying "authentic" Black cultural expression with the masses of Black people. The tone of this aesthetic populism is captured in Maulana Ron Karenga's discussion of "the question of popularization versus elevation":

Our intention is that if art is from the people and for the people, there is no question of raising people to art or lowering art to people, for they are one and the same thing. . . . Art is everyday life given more form and color. And what one seeks to do then is to use art as a means of educating the people, and being educated by them, so that it is mutual exchange rather than a one way communication. Art and people must develop at the same time and for the same reason. It must be with the masses and moved by the masses.[16]

The construction and narration of Black life in Black Aesthetic discourse, then, were to find their sources in the semiotic possibilities inherent in the symbols and forms of ordinary Black life and, above all, to be structured by a dialectical relationship between the artist and "the people." Larry Neal addressed the deconstruction of the artist–people opposition when his call for the destruction of the traditional text was accompanied by a proposal for the creation of a new text. Nothing short of a complete insertion of the work of art into political praxis was acceptable. Arguing that the "artist and political activist are one," he called for the Black artist to aid in the formation of a collective Black consciousness "that would destroy dead useless ideas . . . affirm our highest possibilities, and yet be honest with us."[17]

Since Neal maintained that the highest form of Black ritual expression was in popular culture, he argued that the responsibility of the artist was to reverse the oppositions written/oral, literary/nonliterary, high culture/popular culture. To achieve this end, artists were to assume roles as both entertainers and political activists. Commenting on these functions, Neal wrote:

The poet must become a performer the way James Brown is a performer—loud, gaudy, and racy. He must take his work where the people are: Harlem, Watts, Philadelphia, Chicago, and the rural South. He must learn to embellish the context in which work is executed, and where possible, link the work to all aspects of music. . . . Poets must learn to sing, chant, and dance their works, tearing into the substance of their individual and collective experiences. We must make literature move people to a deeper understanding of what this thing is all about, be a kind of priest, a black magician, working juju with the world on the world.[18]

This emphasis on a dialectical interplay of artist, text, and community was strongly in evidence in the construction of street theater as a mode of fictive discourse. Ed Bullins, a playwright and spokesperson for the Black Aesthetic movement, proposed this approach to the production of drama for the consumption of the Black masses:

Short, sharp incisive plays are best. Contemporary themes, satirical pieces on current counter-revolutionary figures or enemies of the people, humorous themes, also children's plays with revolutionary lessons are good street play material. Also starting unique material, something that gives the masses identifying images, symbols, and challenging situations. Each individual in the crowd should have his sense of reality confronted, his consciousness assaulted.[19]

Black Aesthetic discourse, then, was largely structured by semiotic strategies by which the signs of Black life were reflected and refracted. These signs were then to be further transformed by the artist into myths through which the Black masses were to be "interpellated"[20] and thereby moved to political consciousness. A general structuring of racial identity and a heightening of political consciousness were seen as the desired results of this new definition and fusion of aesthetic and political practice.

Roles of Black Women

If the semiotic strategies of Black Aesthetic discourse was primarily focused on constructing alternative and oppositional modes of signification to those of the dominant (white) culture, a problematic aspect of that discourse was its representation of Black women. Largely determined by the ideological doctrine of Black Power, and therefore largely male-centered, Black Aesthetic discourse represented the political struggle as exclusively the domain of Black men.

Political theorist Manning Marable pointed out that the nationalists' position regarding the primacy of Black family survival superseded the desires and needs of Black women. Citing the emphasis on "femininity" and submission that characterized Karenga's and Baraka's descriptions of the roles of women in the struggle against racism, Marable argued that even the most personal aspects of women's lives were under male control. He describes a pronouncement on Black women's sexuality by the nationalist poet Haki Madhubuti (Don L. Lee):

The options for Black women were unpleasant. Going "without Black men," or sexual abstinence was "unnatural and against life." Homosexual activity among women was abnormal, "for it does not generate reproduction with the opposite sex," and the prospect of Black women/white men's sexual relationship was particularly offensive (because) there is a serious consequence of genocide.[21]

This political position was variously reproduced in cultural texts. In the works of Baraka, Bullins, Neal, and others, three approaches inform the representation of women: the Black woman suppressed in the text and largely signified by her absence, the Black woman as traitor to the more progressive nationalist forces, and the reified Black woman as goddess or

as symbol of an African queen. This last construction is illustrated in a passage from one of Neal's poems:

> Black women, timeless, are sun breaths
> are crying mothers
> are snatched rhythms
> are blues rivers and food uncooked
> lonely villages beside quiet streams,
> are exploding suns green yellow moons,
> the story of the snake and turtle.
> lonely roads.
> night-rider. see-see rider; easy men
> who got lost returning to you,
> blues in our mothers' voices
> warming us.
> blues people bursting out.
> Like it is, I tell it.
> and there are towns that
> hang lonely in some man's
> memory and you are there
> and not there.[22]

Representations of women as pervasive signifiers of nationalist culture (e.g., the tranquil African existence represented
in the equation of women with "sun breaths" and "snatched
rhythms") were dominant constructions of Black women in
Black Aesthetic texts. These representations, occurring far too
often to enumerate here, were extensively produced throughout much of the period.

An important one-act play that reproduces the major ideological formulations of the time was Jimmie Garrett's *And We
Own the Night*. Initially performed in 1967 at a rally for Huey
Newton and the Black Panther party at the Fillmore Audito-
rium in San Francisco, it attracted a large audience, including
such key figures of the Black Nationalist movement as Stokely
Carmichael, H. Rap Brown, and Bobby Seales. The play's
later inclusion in several "revolutionary" anthologies of drama
in the 1960s achieved for it significant status among texts of
Black nationalist discourse.

The protagonist of *And We Own the Night* is Johnny, a teenage Black male who becomes a hero by killing a white policeman; later, Johnny shoots his own mother during an uprising in a Black ghetto. The play engages its audience through a rather heavyhanded inscription of signs and representations that are central to nationalist ideology. Urban violence is encoded as "insurrection"; the "doctor," identified only by his fair complexion and middle-class status, is the embodiment of racial inauthenticity; the violence of Black youths is represented as heroic; and the act of matricide is justified politically as the symbolic destruction of a repressive matriarchy. Ironically, this representation of the Black mother as destructive echoes a similar myth in the dominant discourse. Although such a representation could have become a problem, Neal justified it artistically and politically when he wrote this critique of the play:

In Afro-American literature of previous decades, the strong Black mother was the object of awe and respect. In the new literature her status is one of ambivalence and tension. . . . [In the past] the woman's aspirations [were] closely tied to those of the white power structure and not to those of her man. Since he cannot provide for his family the way white men do, she despises his weakness, tearing into him every opportunity until, very often, there is nothing left but a shell.[23]

The Emergence of Black Feminist Consciousness

The complex relationship between Black Aestheticians and their audiences, essentially grounded in semiosis, evokes Stephen Greenblatt's concept of an "improvisational mode"— that is, "the ability to transform given materials into one's own scenario." He further asserts that this improvisation "depends upon the willingness to transform oneself, if only for a brief period and with mental reservations, into another." He concludes that if "improvisation is made possible by the subversive perception of another's truth as an ideological construct, that construct must at the same time be grasped in terms that bear a certain structural resemblance to one's own set of beliefs." [24] Central to the act of self-fashioning, this mode of improvisation represents to a large extent the processes of cultural production that structured Black Aesthetic discourse. The enabling element in the emergence of Black consciousness was a specific ideological environment in which signs proliferated. Black nationalist artists and theorists appropriated the signs, made them central to self-definition, and constructed myths of Black nationalism that they then narrated.

Only with the waning of the civil rights and Black Power movements in the mid 1970s did the Black Aesthetic movement significantly decline. Perhaps an even more important development, however, was the emergence of a Black feminist consciousness that would deconstruct and rewrite Black Aesthetic texts. The blind spots of a largely male discourse would be illuminated, and Black Aesthetic discourse would be modified to accommodate Black feminist desire.

TWO

◆

Enabling Discourse for
Afro-American Women Writers

THE BROAD-BASED political movement that provided the context for the Black Aesthetic did not exist for Black feminist discourse. In the 1960s, race became the overriding sign for all Black oppression. This subjection of Black feminist discourse to the politics of race had a largely negative impact on the production, distribution, and reception of literature written by Black women. Barbara Smith, addressing this issue, argued:

The fact that a parallel Black feminist movement has been much slower in evolving cannot help but have an impact upon the situation of Black women writers and artists and explains in part why during this very same period we have been so ignored. There is no political movement to give power or support to those who want to examine Black women's experience through studying our history, literature, and culture. There is no political presence that demands a minimum level of consciousness and respect from those who write or talk about our lives. Finally, there is not a developed body of Black feminist political theory whose assumptions could be used in the study of Black women's art.[1]

It was not solely the absence of a political presence and the suppression of an alternative voice that impeded the emergence of Black feminist literature. Equally significant was Black women's relationship to the civil rights struggle and the emer-

gent liberal white feminist movement of the 1960s and 1970s.
The agenda of Black male activists dominated the political
questions focused on race. Moreover, the formation of the
National Organization for Women and the publication of Betty
Friedan's *The Feminine Mystique*, while signifying the emerging
consciousness of white feminists, significantly failed to address
issues related to Black women.[2]

The ideological tensions generated by conflicts between
Black women and white feminists, as well as Black males, are
addressed in the Combahee River Collective statement. This
treatise, prepared by a group of Black feminists, speaks to the
disempowerment of Black women in both the Black liberation
movement and feminist politics.

Black feminist politics [had] an obvious connection in and for black
liberation movements, particularly those of the 1960s and 1970s.
Many of us were active in those movements . . . and all our lives
were affected and changed by their ideology, their goals, and the
tactics used to achieve their goals. It was our experience and disillusionment within these liberation movements, as well as experience
on the periphery of the white male left, that led to the need to develop a politics that was antiracist, unlike those of white women,
and antisexist, unlike those of Black and white men.[3]

Thus, Black feminist discourse is fraught with ideological
complexities. Central to its formation is identification with
and opposition to the discursive formations generated by the
racial politics of Black males and the gender politics of white
females. Members of the collective elaborate:

Although we are feminists and lesbians, we feel solidarity with progressive Black men and do not advocate the fractionalization that
white women who are separatists demand. Our situation as Black
people necessitates that we have solidarity around the fact of race,
which white women, of course, do not need to have with white men,
unless it is their negative solidarity as racial oppressors. We struggle
together with Black men against racism, while we also struggle with
Black men about sexism. (Pp. 356–366)

The fusion of race and gender issues in Black feminist discourse results in textual production that is far more complex than that of Black nationalist or liberal feminist texts. The emergence of a specific Black feminist consciousness is at its roots akin to Lucien Goldmann's concept of genetic structuralism. Addressing the transformations characteristic of emergent consciousness, Goldmann wrote:

All human behavior is an attempt to give a meaningful response to a particular situation and tends, therefore, to create a balance between the subject of action and the object on which it bears the environment. . . .

Human relations are presented as two-sided processes: destructuration of old structurations and structurations of new totalities capable of creating equilibria capable of satisfying the new demands of the social groups that are elaborating them.[4]

For Goldmann, the processes of "destructuration" and "restructuration" occur within a context in which individuals always belonged to several groups (e.g., family, nation, race), each acting on his or her consciousness to form a "unique, complex, and relatively incoherent structure." When the group comes into a consciousness of its own, however, memberships in other units tend to cancel one another out and "we are confronted with a much simpler, more coherent structure."[5]

I would argue that what emerges in Black feminist discourse in general and the narratives of Black women in particular is probably less a "simpler, more coherent structure" than a discursive formation marked by tensions and dissonance; however, Goldmann's concepts of "destructuration" and "restructuration" seem central to the production of texts generated in a political context that is both race and gender specific.

The Combahee Statement illuminates the race-gender problematic in Black feminist discourse. As self-named lesbian–feminists, the members of the collective opposed homophobia along with racism and sexism. Racial politics, however, precluded total identification with sexual politics.

Arguing that the perceived anti-male bias of the politics of lesbian separatism omits "far too much and far too many people,
particularly Black men, women, and children," the Combahee women explicitly stated their opposition to, and difference
from, the politics of lesbian separatism:

> We reject the stance of lesbian separatism because it is not a viable
> political analysis or strategy for us. We have a great deal of criticism
> and loathing for what men have been socialized to be in this society,
> what they support, how they act, and how they oppress. But we do
> not have the misguided notion that it is their maleness, per se . . .
> that makes them what they are. As Black women we find any type
> of biological determinism a particularly dangerous and reactionary
> basis upon which to build a politic. We must also question whether
> lesbian separatism is an adequate and progressive political analysis
> and strategy . . . since it so completely denies any but sexual sources
> of women's oppression, negating the facts of race and class. (P. 367)

One might expect, then, that the narratives of Black
women are almost always driven by ideological positions that
are essentially dissonant and at times even contradictory. If we
read the political text, or more accurately the historical moment of their production, we are able to identify the tensions
that inform their creation.

The Reconceptualization of Feminist Discourse

Discussion of the narrative strategies employed by Black
women writers properly begins with an exploration of their
semiotic practices. The racial dimension of Afro-American
women's fiction may be traced to Black Aesthetic discourse,
but the insertion of a Black female subject requires extensive
revision of that discourse. Not only the rewriting of the racial
narrative but a significant reconceptualization of feminist discourse would be needed to accommodate the politics of race.
The intricate restructuring of narrative priorities in the representation of experience necessary to such a revision is rather
like Sandra Gilbert and Susan Gubar's description of the rela-

tionship of the woman writer to patriarchal discourse in general. Addressing the issues central to a woman's narrating her story, they write:

Her battle . . . is not against her (male) precursor's reading of the world but against his reading of her. In order to define herself as an author she must redefine the terms of her socialization. Her revisionary struggle, therefore, often becomes a struggle for what Adrienne Rich has called "Revision—the act of looking back, of seeing with fresh eyes, of entering an old text from a new critical direction . . . an act of survival."[6]

Gilbert and Gubar conclude by arguing that women writers "actively seek a female precursor who . . . proves by example that a revolt against patriarchal literary authority is possible."[7] Directions in Black feminist criticism in general have rediscovered Zora Neale Hurston as a female precursor. Nevertheless, one should be mindful of the dangers inherent in postulating too hastily the existence of a "tradition" of Afro-American women's narrative. Hazel Carby's recent discussion of Black feminist criticism illuminates the problems inherent in such a critical approach:

Black feminist criticism has too frequently been reduced to an experiential relationship that exists between black women as critics and black women as writers who represent black women's reality. Theoretically, this reliance on a common, or shared, experience is essentialist and ahistorical. Following the methodologies of mainstream literary criticism and feminist literary criticism, black feminist criticism presupposes the existence of a tradition and has concentrated on establishing a narrative of that tradition. This narrative constitutes a canon from these essentialist views of experience which is then placed alongside, though unrelated to, traditional and feminist canons.[8]

Although I do not argue for the creation or construction of a Black women's narrative "tradition" that has its genesis in Hurston's fiction, or even that her work might be read as a model for Black women's writing, I do suggest that an examination of her textual strategies significantly clarifies the problems characteristic of race- and gender-specific narratives.

The Narrative Strategies of Zora Neale Hurston

Hurston wrote during the Harlem Renaissance and the Great Depression, two moments in history when Black letters were dominated by male voices, and a politicized Black male discourse focused on racial oppression. Introducing a female subject and proto-feminist discourse, Hurston focused on the deconstruction of privileged and valorized epistemologies and the substitution of alternative feminine perceptions. Whereas the dominant view favored science, Hurston praised folk wisdom. Black male narratives focused on the public arena and racial strife; Hurston stressed the private and domestic. And whereas Black male narratives addressed the struggles between an inner Black world and an outer white world, Hurston largely restricted her explorations to the inner world of Black life.[9]

Hurston's deconstructive strategies signaled a political and cultural intervention essentially different from the dominant racial discourse of the period. Those who claimed the right to address racial issues were more or less in harmony with the position Wright articulated in "Blueprint," and the issues Hurston raised were largely discredited. The two discursive formations—Black male writers' emphasis on racial struggle and Hurston's on the private and personal—are distinguished in much the same way as Michel Foucault's "subjugated and scientific knowledges."

By subjugated knowledges one should understand . . . a whole set of knowledges that have been disqualified as inadequate to their task or insufficiently elaborated; naive knowledges, located low down on the hierarchy, beneath the required level of cognition or scientificity. I believe that it is through the reemergence of these low ranking knowledges, these unqualified even disqualified knowledges . . . and which I would call a popular knowledge (*le savoir de gens*) though it is far from being a general commonsense knowledge, but is on the contrary a particular, local, regional knowledge, a differential knowledge incapable of unanimity and which owes its force only to the harshness with which it is opposed by everything surrounding it —that it is through the reappearance of this knowledge . . . that criticism performs its work.[10]

Hurston undermines scientific knowledge by emphasizing subjugated forms of knowledge, a strategy that is clearly evident in her approach to anthropological chores. When Hurston "does" anthropology, nothing separates the anthropologist and the subject of her inquiry; she strongly emphasizes, sometimes explicitly and other times implicitly, the relationship between the two. We observe in her work the fusion of Geertz's notion of the "experience-near" and the "experience-distant" approaches to anthropological research.[11]

In one of the first deconstructive readings of Hurston's works, Barbara Johnson addresses Hurston's "strategies and structures of problematic address" and manner of "dealing with multiple agendas and heterogeneous implied readers."[12] Arguing that Hurston alternately narrates from an "inside" and an "outside," Johnson considers a passage from *Mules and Men*:

The shifts and reversals in this passage are multiple. Hurston begins as an outsider, a scientific narrative voice that refers to "these people" in the third person, as a group whose inner lives are difficult to penetrate. Then, suddenly, she leaps into the picture she has just painted, including herself in a "we" that addresses a "you" —the white reader, the new implied outsider. The structure of address changes from description to direct address. From that point on it is impossible to tell whether Hurston the narrator is *describing* a strategy or *employing* one.[13]

This rather intricate narrative strategy becomes even more evident in Hurston's fiction in which the merging of at least two narrative voices produces the text's ideology. Of particular interest is the manner in which a seemingly simple realistic narrative is transformed into a statement of proto-feminist ideology. This process can be seen at work in the modes of narration in *Their Eyes Were Watching God*, generally considered to be one of the earliest statements of Black feminist ideology.

"de mule uh de world"

Their Eyes Were Watching God was produced in a period in which Afro-American fiction, indeed most writing of the time, primarily emphasized the political. In the post-Harlem Renaissance and the Great Depression period, Black writers saw the patronage system decline as a literary mode of production.[14] Wright's "Blueprint" was the earliest expression of concern for the political content of art. And perhaps the most concrete application of Wright's theory to his own works was in two of his early short stories, "Fire and Cloud" and "Bright and Morning Star," both of which focused on the fusion of the ideologies of Black nationalism and Marxism to achieve political power. Other Black writers of the period, while not necessarily Marxist in their orientation, also highlighted issues primarily related to the Black liberation struggle. Arna Bontemps's rereading and reinscription of the Gabriel Prosser slave rebellion in Virginia in 1800 resulted in the reconstruction of that event as a metaphor for the transhistorical Black quest for freedom.[15] William Attaway's novels, with their focus on the cultural dislocation resulting from the shift of the Black population from the rural South to the urban North, from an economy based on agriculture to one in which technology and industry were dominant, and from a politics based on race to one that assumed class as a central element, further contributed to the prevailing trends in fictional development among Black writers during the period.[16]

Produced within this historical and cultural milieu, Hurston's novel was significant for its radical refusal to reproduce the ideologies that informed Black cultural production of the period. *Their Eyes Were Watching God* actually undermines Black writing of the time through its insertion of the feminine. While novels by Black males focused on racial struggles between Blacks and whites, Hurston's novel explored the personal, internal struggles between men and women in the Black community. While her male colleagues represented the heroic and antiheroic exploits of Black males, Hurston focused almost exclusively on the Black woman's quest for personal freedom. And while Black male writers generally viewed Black folklore and the folk tradition as peripheral to the major concerns of their narratives, Hurston saw them as fundamental elements, as constituting dominant existential modalities of Black life, and gave folklore a central role in her narrative.

The ideology of *Their Eyes Were Watching God* is produced through a somewhat intricate narrative process. Janie, the putative narrator, tells her story to Pheoby, who mediates between Janie's world and that of the reader, establishing external frames of references for the issues generated by the narrative. Two voices, articulated in two essentially different linguistic codes, always address the reader and the interplay of these voices produces the ideology of the text. Basil Bernstein's concepts of elaborated and restricted codes might be helpful here. Identifying linguistic codes directly with the social class of speakers, Bernstein defines the elaborated code as that of the middle-class speaker and the restricted code as that of the working class. Bernstein describes their roles:

Elaborated codes orient their users towards universalistic meanings, whereas restricted codes orient, sensitize their users to particularistic meanings. . . . Elaborated codes are less tied to a given or local structure and thus contain the potentiality of change in principles. . . . When codes are elaborated the socialised has more access to the grounds of his own socialisation and so can enter into reflexive relationship to the social order he has taken over. Where codes are restricted, the socialised has less access to the grounds of his socialisation, and thus reflexiveness may be limited in range.[17]

Janie and her peers employ a subliterate linguistic mode largely represented by its evocation of Black speech patterns.

Marked by its identification with a rural Black folk culture, it establishes the difference between its world and that of the reader. (My assumption here, of course, is that the reading public is largely middle class and white.) This code, which often depends on parable and metaphor, situates Hurston's characters in the realm of the exotic, the racially and culturally different. Thus their discourse—represented by the particular and concrete and hermetically enclosed within a specific Black culture—allows the reader to distance himself or herself from events in the narrative. The external narrator, however, employs a code that is the same as that of the apparent reader, and through her mediations situates that discourse in another realm, bestowing upon it ideological significance. This narrative ploy can be seen in several key episodes of the novel.

Nanny, Janie's grandmother, concerned about her granddaughter's welfare and recognizing her own suffering, advances an argument for Janie's need to marry:

Honey, de white man is de ruler of every thing as far as Ah been able tuh find out. Maybe it's some place way off in de ocean where de black man is in power, but we don't know nothin' but what we can see. So de white man throw down de load and tell de nigger man tuh pick it up. He pick it up because he have to, but he don't tote it. He hand it to his womenfolks. De nigger woman is de mule uh de world so far as Ah can see. Ah been praying for it to be different with you.[18]

The figure of the Black woman as "de mule uh de world" becomes a dialectical metaphor,[19] subsuming the major episodes and illuminating an aspect of the text's ideology. Nanny enlarges on this metaphor through her personal story when she relates her experience as a victim of sexual exploitation by her white master and recalls the rape of her daughter (Janie's mother). The metaphor, embedded within a parable, also is used to support Nanny's argument for a marriage based on property and security.

For Janie, however, the figure of the "mule" directly conflicts with her metaphors of the pear tree and the horizon. Hence the two figures represent at a colloquial level the tensions that the text seeks to resolve and the ideologies it wishes to explore. Within this context, the narrative remains within the realm of the particular: the conflict between a wise old Black woman and her naive granddaughter. There is still distance between the world of the text and that of the reader.

The external narrator transcodes that conflict, however, restating it in the linguistic framework of the reader. After inserting two rhetorical questions—"Did marriage end the cosmic loneliness of the unmated?" and "Did marriage compel love like the sun of the day?"—she undermines Nanny's position through irony. Describing Janie's impending marriage to Logan Killicks, she observes:

In the few days to live before she went to Logan Killicks and his often-mentioned sixty acres, Janie asked inside of herself and out. She went back and forth to the pear tree continuously wondering and thinking. Finally out of Nanny's talk and her own conjectures, she made a sort of comfort for herself. Yes, she would love Logan after they were married. She could see no way for it to come about, but Nanny and the old folks had said it, so it must be so. Husbands and wives always loved each other, and that was what marriage meant. (P. 38)

Clearly what is foreshadowed here is the failure of the marriage. Even the tone in which the narrator describes Janie's entry into the marriage is ominous ("In the few days in which she had to live," and Killicks's "often-mentioned sixty acres"), and the text from that moment simply moves to illustrate that marriage does not end "the cosmic loneliness of the unmated" or "compel love like the sun of the day." Janie's desire for "things sweet wid mah marriage lak when you sit under a pear tree and think" is destined to go unfulfilled. The failure of the marriage constitutes an epiphany for Janie, but it is the narrator who intervenes to interpret the episode: "The familiar people and things had failed her so she hung over the gate and looked up the road towards way off. She knew now that marriage did not make love. Janie's first dream was dead, so she became a woman" (P. 44).

What occurs in the episodes focused on the union between Logan and Janie, then, is the demystification of marriage as a romantic institution. The mystical and sensuous world of the pear tree stands in direct contrast to the crude reality of marriage as an unromantic institution based on security and property. This ideological statement is reinforced almost entirely through the narrator's mediation, which comments on, enlarges, and interprets Janie's feelings, thereby placing them in a larger context.

The relationship of narrative stance to the production of ideology is far more complex in sections of the text that explore Janie's marriage to Joe Starks. Here the issue is the empowerment of men and the resulting suppression of women's voices. Through complex narrative strategies of irony, direct commentary, and intertextuality, Hurston reinforces the ideology of the text. The tone of this section is announced in the description of the couple on the day of their marriage:

He was very solemn and helped her to the seat beside him. With him on it, it sat like some high, ruling chair. From now on until death she was going to have flower dust and spring time sprinkled over everything. A bee for her bloom. Her old thoughts were going to come in handy now, but new words would have to be made and said to fit them. (Pp. 54–55)

Here the narrator's appropriation of the language and perceptions of the world of the characters encapsulates what will eventually represent the areas of major conflict between Janie and Joe. The ruling chair, representing Joe's need for power and control, will later appear recurrently in the depiction of their marriage as the symbol of male power and dominance, as well as the location from which she is totally objectified. Joe "[builds] a high chair for her to sit and overlook the world," thereby alienating her from the world of real people with whom she wishes to interact. The narrator again contextualizes Janie's position that "we ain't natural wid one 'nother" by broadening its frame of reference:

Janie soon began to feel the impact of awe and envy against her sensibilities. The wife of the mayor was not just another woman as she had supposed. She slept with authority and so was part of it in the town mind. She couldn't get but so close to most of them in spirit. (P. 74)

In at least one point in the narrative, Hurston reintroduces irony to comment on male oppression of women. While Joe's physical abuse of Janie occurs within a particular and personal context, its presentation in the narrative expands it to reflect on the seemingly trivial events that often lead to domestic violence. Focusing on the moment when Janie withdrew from her marriage, the narrator describes the physical attack as follows:

It happened over one of those dinners that chasten all women sometimes. They plan and they fix, and they do, and then some kitchen-dwelling fiend slips a scrochy, soggy, tasteless mess into their pots and pans. Janie was a good cook and Joe had looked forward to his dinner as a refuge from other things. So when the bread didn't rise, and the fish wasn't quite done at the bone, and the rice was scorched, he slapped Janie until she had a ringing sound in her ears. (P. 112)

This narrative establishes a link between Janie and Joe's specific domestic situation and the larger world in which marital discord leads to domestic violence. This linkage of the particular world of Eatonville and the world of the reader is made even more forcefully when the narrator intervenes to explain the impact of Janie's verbal triumph over Joe in the "signifying" contest. What is at issue is not only the intervention of a woman in a largely male ritual but the status of manhood itself. The narrator then interprets the encounter for the reader, placing it in a broader context and thereby connecting it with a world that is recognizable to the reader:

Janie had robbed him of his illusion of irresistible maleness that all men cherish, which was terrible. The thing that Saul's daughter had done to David. But Janie had done worse, she had cast down his empty armor before men and they had laughed and would keep on laughing. When he paraded his possessions hereafter, they would not consider the two together. (P. 123)

The verbal exchange is then removed from its lighthearted context and, through the narrator's mediation, becomes a metaphor for large issues of the code of manliness and a direct statement of male–female relationships. Throughout those episodes of the novel that focus on the union between Janie and Joe, there is a recurrent intertextuality, a strategy in which much of the material from Hurston's other works is retextualized and appears as embedded narratives. These appearances in their new contexts give the material larger metaphorical significance. All the bawdiness of the lying sessions is reproduced here, but it assumes special significance because it represents a world of male camaraderie from which women are excluded, and the incident of the mule, taken from *Mule Bone*, the collaborative effort between Hurston and Langston Hughes,[20] becomes an extended metaphor, reinvoking Nanny's original metaphor and indirectly commenting on Janie's marital situation. The anthropological materials, commented on and illuminated by the external narrator, are reworked within the context of the novel as tropes through which the underlying ideology of the text is explored. This transcoding of materials from the restricted code to the metalanguage of elaborate codes demands that the reader confront its ideology.

The narrator's intervention is even more direct in her exploration of Janie's internal conflict, the tensions between the "inside" and the "outside." Because Janie "didn't read books," her sense of self-worth is diminished (P. 119). This direct separation between Janie and the reader justifies a narrative intervention in which the narrator interprets Janie's life for us. Still, in carefully remaining within the world of Eatonville and simultaneously taking a position outside it, the narrator mediates between text and reader. The language of the narrator, although increasingly metaphorical, is couched in the code of the reader without dramatically removing itself from the Eatonville milieu.

Hence the inside–outside dichotomy (which represents the private and public sides of Janie's life) and the image of Janie's starching and ironing her face (which represents her acting out public roles) keep the text grounded in the epistemology of the concrete material world. And as metaphorical vehicles, they enable the reader to grasp the ideological content of the text, thus reinforcing it. An example of this strategy is seen in Hurston's treatment of the encounter between Janie and Joe in the store. Joe, sensitive about his physical degeneration, attempts to ridicule and degrade Janie by disparaging her physical appearance. At the conclusion of his tirade, the narrator interprets the crowd's response:

A big laugh started off in the store but people got to thinking and stopped. It was funny if you looked at it right quick, but it got pitiful if you thought about it awhile. It was like somebody snatched off part of a woman's clothes while she wasn't looking and the streets were crowded. Then too, Janie took the middle of the floor to talk right into Jody's face, and that was something hadn't been done before. (P. 122)

This direct address to the reader—"It was funny if you looked at it right quick, but it got pitiful if you thought about it awhile"—elicits a reexamination of the episode and the insertion of it within the broader ideological framework of the novel. An event that, unmediated, seemed like raucous humor among "primitive" Blacks, is metaphorically expanded to represent the dehumanizing of Janie. The movement from Janie in particular to a woman in general ("It was like somebody snatched off part of a woman's clothes") even more strongly demands that the incident be read as a metaphor for the degradation of all women.

The narrative strategy in the section of the novel that focuses on Janie's union with Joe, then, is always determined by the ideology of the text. Through a complex interplay between elaborate and restricted codes, the particular and often seemingly exotic is transmuted and reconstructed as a metaphor for larger issues. Here the narrative intervention is more direct than in the treatment of Janie's union with Killicks because the issues involved—the powerlessness of women and the dominance of men—are considerably more complex. While the Killicks episode simply deconstructed the mythology of marriage as a romantic institution, the Starks episode explores it as the site of women's oppression.

The third division of the text, those episodes in which the dominant focus is the union between Janie and Tea Cake, involves still more complex narrative strategies. The apparent unifying focus is the marriage itself, representing Janie's discovery of both her pear tree and horizon, and thereby evoking the ideal nonoppressive representation of marriage. Yet in this section of the novel the most radical departures from the novel's concerns are introduced. Not only does a subtext undermine the romantic depiction of marriage, but narrative boundaries collapse as political issues are inserted into the text.

On the surface, an idyllic union is constructed. Janie abandons the world of property and responsibility to embark on the carefree life promised by a union with Tea Cake. Her act marks not only an assertion of freedom but a dramatic break with her past. It becomes a total repudiation of Nanny's view, which valued "property and titles." Rejecting Nanny's position on the grounds that "Ah done live Grandma's way, now Ah means tuh live mine," Janie explains to her friend Pheoby:

She was borned in slavery when folks, dat is black folks, didn't sit down anytime dey felt lak it. So sittin' on porches lak de white madam looked lak uh mighty fine thing tuh her. Dat's what she wanted for me—don't keer whut it cost. Git up on uh high chair and sit dere. She didn't have time tuh think whut tuh do after you got up on de stool uh do nothin'. De object wuz tuh git dere. So Ah got up on de high stool lak she told me, but Pheoby, Ah done nearly languished tuh death up dere. Ah felt like de world wuz cryin' extry and Ah ain't read de common news yet. (P. 173)

This statement of rebellion summarizes the failure of the first two marriages and signals the emergence of Janie's new consciousness. The "high chair" and "high stool" metaphors point even more specifically to the union with Starks and reemphasize for the reader the particular failures of that marriage. It projects an ideal picture of marriage in Janie's union with Tea Cake. Yet central to that union is an emphasis on an uncomplicated life marked by the couple's working together in the fields, indulging in sensual pleasures, and participating in the various rituals—parties, lying sessions—that are part of an organic Black community. Even those moments of jealousy that the couple experiences are initially represented in a light manner. In presenting this idyllic picture of marriage, however, the text glides over some of the problems with the union, seeming to move away from its own ideology.

This is evident when Tea Cake beats Janie "tuh show dem Turners who is boss." The narrator intervenes to place the incident in context from Tea Cake's point of view:

When Mrs. Turner's brother came and she brought him over to be introduced, Tea Cake had a brainstorm. Before the week was over he had whipped Janie. Not because her behavior justified his jealousy, but it relieved that awful fear inside him. Being able to whip her reassured him in possession. No brutal beating at all. He just slapped her around a bit to show he was boss. Everybody talked about it next day in the fields. It aroused a sort of envy in both men and women. (P. 218)

The narrative perspective employed raises two important points. In the previous description of Joe Starks's slapping Janie, the narrator's tone is one of strong disapproval and the focus is clearly on Janie's response, signaling the point in her marriage when she could no longer be "petal blossom" open with Joe. The shift to Tea Cake's perspective, the trivializing of the incident in the text ("No brutal beating at all. He just slapped her around a bit to show he was boss."), and the suppression of Janie's voice result in an ideological ambiguity.

The description of the community's approval and envy would indicate that Hurston is describing a culture in which violence against women was normal. Most significant is the narrator's refusal to judge the act or represent it in a manner that would make Tea Cake a villain or an unsympathetic character.

This episode might be seen as one of several in which both the narrative focus and resultant ideology of the text become less clearly delineated than they are in earlier sections of the novel. New thematic materials are introduced that signal two forms of disruption: deconstructions of the previously depicted organic black communities and the overall apparent unity of the text. While the episodes that depict the union between Tea Cake and Janie suggest a surface ideological closure and resolution, the materials in the subtext highlight dissonances and contradictions.

An example of this is seen in the representation of Mrs. Turner in the text. The introduction of the political issue of "colorism" inserts an issue peripheral to the dominant ideology of the text. Mrs. Turner's scorn for blacks, depicted at the level of caricature, is symbolic of the self-hatred that some light-complexioned blacks experience. Her rejection of everything black: "White doctors always gits mah money. Ah don't go in no nigger store tuh buy nothin' neither. Colored folks don't know nothin' bout no business" (p. 211) and her celebration of her own white features ("Look at me! Ah ain't got no flat nose and liver lips. Ah'm uh featured woman" [p. 211]) make her a figure for ridicule. The narrator, however, depicts her as a comic–tragic figure:

Mrs. Turner, like all other believers, had built an altar to the un-attainable—Caucasian characteristics for all. Her god would smite her, would hurl her from pinnacles and lose her in deserts. But she would not forsake his altars. Behind her crude words was a belief that somehow she and others through worship could attain her paradise —a heaven of straight-haired, thin-lipped, high-nose bone white seraphs. (P. 216)

The introduction of color strife within the black community serves two purposes in the text. First, it reinforces the image of Janie as both maverick and heroic figure. As a fair-complexioned black, she chooses to identify with ordinary blacks, thus manifesting what Alice Walker later describes as "racial health." This depiction of Janie resonates with Hurston's larger battle with her contemporaries in that it addresses, at least indirectly, the absurdity of denying one's racial identity and seeking total absorption into white culture. Second, it is a deconstruction and rejection of the myth of the tragic mulatta. The mulatta figure, inscribed in previous literature as the embodiment of refinement and heroism, surfaces here as both comic and pathetic.[21]

The hurricane episode introduces still another issue that seems to be extraneous to the major theme of the text: the oppressive relationship between the white world and the black world. Whereas the focus on Janie emphasized intraracial conflict, the shift to Tea Cake addresses the ideology of racism. In this section of the novel, the white world looms as a destructive and omnipresent force, which shapes Tea Cake's understanding of his survival within a racist society. Complaining to Janie about the need to try to reach the Everglades, where they are known by whites, Tea Cake argues:

[In Palm Beach] De [blacks] de white man know is nice colored folks De ones he don't know is bad niggers. . . .

Ah done watched it time and time again; each and every white man think he know all de good darkies already. He don't need tuh know no mo'. So far as he's concerned, all dem he don't know oughta be tried and sentenced tuh six months behind de United States privy house at hard smellin'. (P. 255)

Only limited attention is given to this episode, but it introduces the issue of racial politics into the text. Tea Cake's encounter with whites is always depicted as degrading and dehumanizing. Through the inscription of this dehumanization

and degradation, Hurston moves the text from its major focus
—Janie's coming to womanhood and self-awareness—to the
oppressive relationship between the Black community and the
white community. Again the novel, inserting an alternative
discourse, transgresses its predetermined narrative boundaries.

The major episode in which this shift in narrative focus
occurs is at Janie's trial. Janie, whose guilt or innocence is
to be determined by "twelve strange white men," is presented
as also having to contend with the bigotry of the Black community, which would demand that she pay with her life for
having killed Tea Cake in self-defense. Indicating the force
of the opposition that Janie faces, the narrator represents the
community as a single voice:

Tea Cake was a good boy. He had been good to that woman. No
nigger woman ain't never been treated no better. Naw suh! He
worked like a dog for her and nearly killed himself saving her in the
storm, then soon as he got a little fever from the water, she had
took up with another man. Sent for him to come there from way
off. Hanging was too good. All they wanted was a chance to testify.
(P. 276)

The response replicates earlier reactions to Janie's digressions from community mores—Nanny's disapproval of Janie's
rejection of Logan Killicks, the response of the Eatonville citi-
zenry to her rebellion against Joe Starks, and her initial romantic involvement with Tea Cake. Essentially different here is the
construction of the entire community as a monolothic voice,
the reification and objectification of communal opposition.
The intolerance of the community to women, especially Janie,
who depart from its codes of acceptable conduct is thereby
reinforced.

These seemingly extraneous matters—the colorism issue,
the Black–white conflict, and intolerance in the community
—all appear to disrupt the unity of the text, but they represent
narrative ruptures generated by an attempt to structure an
ideological position from both race and gender concerns.

These episodes relate to problems that must be explored in any attempt to construct Black feminist discourse. As I later illustrate, at least two of the three issues are inscribed in the narratives of Morrison, Bambara, and Walker. Their fiction consists of the significant reconceptualizing, revising, and rewriting of earlier texts. Its racial content is grounded in the proto-nationalism of Wright's early works and the heterogeneous discourses that constitute the Black Aesthetic. Inasmuch as racial discourses construct race around the sign of the Black male, however, the Black female subject becomes the major thrust of Black women's narratives. Central to their strategy is a self-construction that begins with the realization that they are divided between two political imperatives: a politics of race that often suppresses issues of gender, and a politics of gender that marginalizes racial issues. Narrative becomes a vehicle for synthesis and the construction of a new political vision. Such a self-construction inevitably involves the search for alternative modes of narration.

THREE

◆

Racial Discourse, Aesthetics, and Desire in Morrison's *The Bluest Eye* and *Sula*

CRITICAL ANALYSES of Toni Morrison's work have three major focuses. Discussion of form in her novels has led to identifications of patterns of imagery, recurrent metaphors, and what is often cited as Morrison's lyricism. A second critical approach is concerned with the aesthetic texture of Morrison's narratives and their significance as semiotic statements that reproduce realistically a broad construct of Afro-American culture. A central presupposition of that approach is that Morrison's fiction evokes Afro-American folklore and Afro-American mythology, as well as recodings of Black oral traditions.

Moreover, thematic readings suggest that the examination of form and the underlying Afro-American mythology reveals the ideology underpinning Morrison's narratives. The critic generally holds that the raw material of the Morrison narrative—its sources in an anterior Black reality—supports an epistemological framework in which an authentic Black life, represented by that which is harmonious with this mythical Black world, is opposed to inauthentic life, embodied in disharmonious or conflicting elements.

While criticism is invariably structured by ideological positions of individual critics, these concerns, in one variation or another and sometimes simultaneously present in a single "reading" of Morrison, generally enter into the criticism focused on her works. Much of this critical attention interprets the works as nonproblematic bodies of fiction and infers a univocal meaning. Complexities of narrative focus, seeming contradictions in character representations, and ideological dissonance are ignored.[1]

The critic Barbara Christian is exceptional in this regard. Christian's approach to Morrison employs elements of all three standard interpretive strategies. However, she also argues for more detailed examinations of Morrison's narratives, emphasizing their relationship to the lived experiences of Black women and to the body of writings by Afro-American women. In her pioneer study of Black women writers,[2] Christian reads Morrison's novels as powerful delineations of Afro-American life and culture. Viewing them as narratives in which content and form merge to produce significant social documents and profound artistic achievements, she argues:

Toni Morrison's works are fantastic earthy realism. Deeply rooted in history and mythology, her works resonate with mixtures of pleasure and pain, wonder and horror. Primal in their essence, her characters come at you with the force of gushing water, seemingly fantastic but basic as the earth they stand on. They erupt out of the world, sometimes gently, often with force and terror. Her work is sensuality combined with an intrigue that only a piercing intellect could create. (BWN, 137)

Christian views Morrison's aesthetic craft as addressing specific issues related to feminine desire. Of the ideological significance of Morrison's novels, Christian states:

Because Morrison's probings are so relentless, her sounds so authentic, and her appreciation of complexity so profound, we are able to recognize, as do Claudia and Nel, the patterning of beauty and waste in the history of Pecola and Sula and their communities. As a result, *The Bluest Eye* and *Sula* teach us a lesson about the integral relationship between the destructive limits imposed on the Black woman and the inversions of truth in this society. (BWN, 179)

This emphasis on semiosis in Morrison's works, the representations of history and mythology, the symbolic construction of community that results in artistic complexity and, significantly, evocations of the "real" lives of Black women, is central to Christian's reading. Although she explores these issues more extensively in her most recent publication,[3] her focus remains on Morrison's symbolic construction of a community in which the desires of Black women are seldom realized and often frustrated.

Christian argues that the "relationship between Nature and a particular community is the kernel of the contemporary fable as Morrison has wrought it" (BFC, 47). She explores the mythical representation of community in *The Bluest Eye*, *Sula*, and *Song of Solomon*. Although her argument is often complicated by the shifting use of the word *nature*,[4] Christian views location ("place") as the privileged trope in Morrison's writings: "Worlds that are very much like villages are woven into the dreams, the legends, the subconscious of the inhabitants." She continues:

That is why we are first introduced in these novels to the place that the characters inhabit, the land of the community. Like the ancestral tradition, place is as important as the human actors, for the land is the participant in the folk tradition. It is one of the necessary constants through which the folk dramatize the meaning of life, as it is passed on from one generation to the next. Setting, then, is organic to the characters' view of themselves. And a change in place drastically alters the traditional values that give life their coherence. (BFC, 48)

Examining Morrison's three early novels, Christian argues that Pauline Breedlove's tragedy may be partially attributed to her social and spiritual dislocation: "Separated from her the rural South, which allowed her privacy and freedom of imagination, and cut off from the tradition of her maternal ancestors, she falls prey to the destructive ideas of physical beauty and romantic love as measures of self-worth" (BFC, 48). In the discordant relationship between Sula and her community, and in that community's decoding of Nature, Christian identifies an essential tension in the narrative:

> As woman [Sula's] desire to make herself rather than others goes against the most basic principle of the community's struggle to survive. Since she does not fit the image of mother, the loose woman, or the lady-wife as Eva, Hannah, and Helene do, the community relegates her to their other category for woman, that of the witch, the evil conjure woman who is part of the evil forces of Nature. In spite of their attitude toward Sula, the community does not expel her. Rather, it uses her, in spite of herself, for its own sake, as a pariah, as a means of reaffirming their oneness as community. (*BFC*, 54)

Christian extends her analysis to *Song of Solomon*, observing that Macon Dead's "view of Nature" is "representative of a rising middle-class, is to own it, rather than to live within it" and that the "importance of possession applies not only to Nature, but to his family as well." In contrast, Pilate represents "the tradition that identifies with nature, [having] no desire for material things." Pilate's achievements transcend those of Sula because "Pilate is able to do what Sula could not. She embodies the tradition of her family, of the southern community in which she originated, even as she makes herself" (*BFC*, 55).

Highlighting the feminine and the tensions between community needs and feminine desire, Christian provides the context for a more extended ideological analysis of Morrison's works, one that explores more fully the dialectical relationship between form and content in those novels, the extent to which preeminence of the aesthetic and the narrative structure of the works result in an apparent dissonance.

Central to the Morrison narrative is the construction of an ethnic community reinforced by a consciousness of the aesthetic as a textual dominant.[5] The aesthetic, according to James Kavanagh, designates "those ensembles of effects" encountered by the reader that occur "in the space of contact

between a set of writing gestures (*écriture*) and a reading gaze
—a gaze that is itself formed by other texts and practices which
intervene within the gaze to effect a complex, constructive relation that is experienced as if it were a simple 'recognition.' "
Kavanagh strips the aesthetic of its mystification:

We suggest that the aesthetic or the literary–aesthetic identifies a
region of ideological practice. In modern critical discourses, the
"aesthetic" is a sign under which proceed the production and consumption of specific ensembles of effects by ideological practices—
practices that intervene in the subject's sense of a "lived relation
to the real." The literary–aesthetic, then, is not only accompanied
by, but indeed, can only exist as *part of,* an ideological apparatus
whose task is precisely to break certain writing and reading practices
off from others in order to constitute them as "aesthetic," "literary,"
"art," etc. Texts do not exist as aesthetic, except as encrusted in an
"ideology of the aesthetic," or more properly, only so exist as a recognized effect of that ideology, which is no external "encrustation,"
but the very condition of their existence—that which produces them
and which they must reproduce. As Macherey and Balibar suggest:
"Literary is the text recognized as such, and it is recognized as such
precisely in the moment and in the measure that it activates interpretations, criticisms, and readings."[6]

In *The Bluest Eye* and *Sula,* two of Morrison's early works,
the apparent dominance of an "ideology of the aesthetic"
directly conflicts with subtextual eruptions of feminine and
feminist issues. Through complex strategies of representation,
shifts in perspectives, and fragmented stories of feminine or
feminist desire, the Morrison narrative, in spite of its apparent
single voice, is marked by ideological ruptures and dissonance.

Form and the Construction of a Black Community

Morrison's emphasis on form manifests itself through a
conscious framing of the narrative that demands specific interpretations by the reader but also suggests closings and reso-
lutions. Hence, the marigolds as a metaphor and the Dick-

and-Jane narrative in *The Bluest Eye* are textual contrivances
that solicit specific readings of the novel. The Bottom is more
than a geographical place in *Sula*; it is *topos* through which
all actions and characterizations are mediated. And the flying trope in *Song of Solomon*, functioning on both literal and
figurative planes, is the unifying figure for the novel's themes.

In addition to this conscious structuring, Morrison's evocations of folklore, mythology, and Afro-American oral traditions constitute major aspects of her emphasis on form. Select-
ing myths and symbols that underpin Black cultural practices,
she articulated major themes of Afro-American experience.
Form, then, joins with the representation of cultural materials
to produce the myth of an organic Black community.

Morrison, in numerous interviews, has commented on the
processes involved in her fictional constructions.[7] She pre-
sumes a homogeneous Black culture from which she calls materials to construct her fictional worlds. She focuses primarily
on the "village" or the "tribe." Moreover, every minor detail
is considered in terms of its effect before it is incorporated in
her works. The Morrison goal, then, is the construction of
a well-wrought text that portrays a mythical Afro-American
community.

The Bluest Eye

The dominant theme of *The Bluest Eye* is sufficiently transparent that little would be served by an extensive restatement
of it here. Generally read as a masterful achievement in classic
realism,[8] the novel is primarily concerned with the issue of cultural domination, a topic debated extensively in the late 1960s
and early 1970s. It contrasts the "real" life conditions of the
Breedloves and the idealized representation of family life suggested by the dominant ideology in the Dick-and-Jane myth.
The contrast is reinforced by the intervention and mediation
of the narrator, as in the following commentary on the extent
of the Breedlove's oppression.

The Breedloves did not live in a storefront because they were having temporary difficulty adjusting to the cutbacks at the plant. They lived there because they were poor and black, and they stayed there because they believed they were ugly. . . . The master had said, "You are ugly people." They had looked about themselves and saw nothing to contradict the statement; saw in fact, support for it leaning at them from every billboard, every movie, every glance. "Yes," they had said. "You are right." And they took the ugliness in their hands, threw it as a mantle over them, and went about the world with it. Dealing with it each according to his way.[9]

The novel focuses on this characterization and the ideology implied in it. Each episode enlarges on the Breedlove tragedy; minor characters (e.g., Geraldine and Maureen Peal) are introduced to elaborate on this theme. The Dick-and-Jane framework restates it, and the fusion of the first-person narration of Claudia MacTeer with the author's narrative intervention keeps the issue of cultural domination in the foreground.

Critics generally have no difficulty coming to terms with the dominant text. It is, after all, what is there. A restatement of it therefore largely constitutes summary rather than analysis. Nevertheless, a closer reading of the novel might afford a deeper insight into its mode of ideological production. For once the reader resists the aesthetic constraints of the text, he or she is able to recognize those moments of dissonance that disrupt its apparent coherence.

In a rewriting of Benveniste, Catherine Belsey identifies three textual modes predicated on the relationships between text, author, and reader. The declarative text, Belsey argues, imparts " 'knowledge' to a reader whose position is thereby stabilized, through a privileged discourse which is to varying degrees invisible." Exhorting, ordering, and instructing the reader, the imperative text, largely characterized by its association with propaganda, "invites the reader to adopt a position of struggle rather than stability." The interrogative text, marked by its indeterminacy, "invite(s) the reader to produce answers to questions it implicitly or explicitly raises." [10]

Although constructed within a rigid Marxist hermeneu-
tics, focusing on the relationship of the reader as subject in his
or her response to hegemonic texts, Belsey's textual paradigms
are relevant to deconstructive readings of Morrison's works.
Of particular significance is Belsey's identification of classic
realism with the declarative mode:

Classic realism is characterized by *illusionism,* narrative which leads
to closure, and a *hierarchy of discourses* which establish the "truth" of
the story. . . . Narrative tends to follow certain recurrent patterns.
Classic realist narrative, as Barthes demonstrates in S/Z, turns on
the creation of enigma which throws into disarray the conventional
cultural and signifying systems. Among the commonest sources of
disorder at the level of plot in classic realism are murder, war, a journey of love. But the story moves inevitably towards *closure,* which
is also disclosure, the dissolution of enigma through the reestablish-
ment of order, recognizable as reinstatement or a development of the
order which is understood to have preceded the events of the story
itself.[11]

The Bluest Eye develops its dominant themes through the
interplay of two narratives: Claudia MacTeer's rite of passage
and the disintegration of Pecola's life. The novel suggests closure through its exploration of the tragedy of Pecola, mediated
within the frame of the Dick-and-Jane story, and its evocation of the marigold symbol to signify Claudia's passage from
ignorance to knowledge. After Cholly's rape of Pecola, the
disintegration of the Breedlove family, and Pecola's descent
into madness, Claudia reflects on her own narrative and that
of Pecola by locating them within the framework of the opening metaphor and returning to a narrative mode that features
"literary" language:

And now when I see [Pecola] searching the garbage—for what? The
thing we assassinated? I talk about how I did not plant the seed too
deeply, how it was the fault of the earth, the land, our town. I even
think now that the land of the entire country was hostile to marigolds that year. This soil is bad for certain kinds of flowers. Certain

seeds it will not nurture, certain fruit it will not bear, and when the land kills of its own volition, we acquiesce and say the victim had no right to live. We are wrong, of course, but it doesn't matter. It's too late. At least on the edge of my town, among the garbage and the sunflowers of my town, it's much, much, much too late. (P. 160)

Here is the dominance of two hierarchical discourses: the resolution of a *bildungsroman* and a reassertion of a mode of literary discourse in which the focus is on language. The latter strategy constitutes the lyrical quality of Morrison's works. (Consider, for example, the opening of *The Bluest Eye*: "Nuns go by as quiet as lust, and drunken men and sober eyes sing in the lobby of the Greek hotel." This figure is meaningless within the context of the novel and seems almost arbitrary.) On the issue of cultural domination, however, the processes of textualization are even more radically drawn.

Cultural domination is seen as a struggle between two competing discourses: a codification of reality whose legitimacy is asserted (the Dick-and-Jane myth), and an alternative (oppositional) representation that challenges and threatens to displace the first (the "real" story of the Breedloves). The novel illustrates Mikhail Bakhtin's concept of the relationship between authoritative and internally persuasive discourses. Authoritative discourses "embody various contents: authority as such, or the authoritativeness of tradition, of generally acknowledged truths, of the official line and other similar authorities." Of internally persuasive discourse, Bakhtin argues:

When someone else's ideological discourse is internally persuasive for us and acknowledged by us, entirely different possibilities open up. Such discourse is of decisive significance in the evolution of an individual consciousness: consciousness awakens to independent ideological life precisely in a world of alien discourses surrounding it, and from which it cannot initially separate itself; the process of distinguishing between one's own and another's discourse, between one's own and another's thought, is activated rather late in development. When thought begins to work in an independent, experimenting and discriminating way, what first occurs is a separation between internally persuasive discourse and authoritarian enforced discourse, along with a rejection of those congeries of discourses that do not matter to us, that do not touch us.[12]

The Bluest Eye depicts the struggle between two warring factions. The Dick-and-Jane frame has as its referent not only the primer but the cultural values of the dominant society. It is read and deconstructed by the lived experiences of the Breedloves. Juxtapositions of the two narratives not only reinforce the dominant theme of the novel but illuminate the novel's textual processes. Contrasts between the Dick-and-Jane world and the "real" world of the Breedloves are structured around several sets of binary oppositions: White/Black, affluence/poverty, desirability/undesirability, order/chaos, valued/devalued. The "truth" of the authoritative discourse is challenged by the internally persuasive discourse. The comfortable home of the Dick-and-Jane myth is contrasted with the squalid living conditions of the Breedloves; the Dick-and-Jane family has its counterpart in the misery and violence that seem normal among the Breedlove clan; the Dick-and-Jane myth celebrates familial love, while rape and incest are rife in the Breedlove household.

The conflict is transparent, but the focus on the aesthetic and the struggles between the discourses suppress other issues in the text. The resulting text is marked by ideological dissonance and rupture. The dominant themes of the novel become what Fredric Jameson calls "strategies of containment," excluding or suppressing other discourses.[13]

These dominant narrative themes, however, are subverted by embedded narratives that contribute to the overall effect of the book and simultaneously indicate a departure from the novel's primary focus. Although they seem to fill in the Gestalt that constitutes Afro-American culture, they also disrupt the textual dominant emphasis by introducing the problem of feminine desire. This is particularly true in two narratives that inform the ethnographic dimensions of the novel while advancing peripheral materials.

The three prostitutes, China, Poland, and Miss Marie, are casually introduced into the narrative, contributing to the "local color" of the town. Yet they play a much larger part in the text:

They did not belong to those generations of prostitutes created in novels, with greated and generous hearts. . . . Nor were they from that sensitive breed of young girl, gone wrong at the hands of faith. Neither were they sloppy, inadequate whores who, unable to make a living at it alone. . . . Except for Marie's fabled love for Dewy Prince, those women hated men, all men, without shame, apology, or discrimination. Black men, white men, Puerto Ricans, Mexicans, Jews, Poles, whatever—all were inadequate and weak, all came under their jaundiced eyes and were recipients of their disinterested wrath. (Pp. 47–48)

These women have rejected the norms of the community, although they are inscribed in the text as one aspect of "the real" community. But they generate issues that are almost totally unrelated to the novel's dominant focus. What is stressed is their absolute economic and sexual autonomy, the significance of which becomes evident when we examine another group of women:

Everybody in the world was in a position to give them orders. White women said, "Do this." White children said, "Give me that." White men said, "Come here." Black men said, "Lay down." The only people they need not take orders from were black children and each other. But they took all of that and recreated it in their own image. They ran the houses of white people, and knew it. When white men beat their men, they cleaned up the blood and went home to receive abuse from the victim. They beat their children with one hand and stole for them with the other. . . .

Then they were old. Their bodies honed, their odors sour. Squatting in a cane field, stooping in a cotton field, kneeling by a river bank they had, they had carried a world on their heads. . . . [Their] lives were synthesized in their eyes—a puree of tragedy and humor, wickedness and serenity, truth and fantasy. (Pp. 109–110)

These two narratives are readily subsumed by the ideological thrust of the novel through their focus on the feminine, but they create points of rupture in the text. As elements of "real life," they contribute to the total representation of Black culture, but as specific articulations of women's lives, they disrupt the novel's focus on the struggle between authoritative and internally persuasive discourses. The prostitutes embody women's independence and empowerment, while Aunt Jenny's peers, largely a reproduction of Hurston's characterization of Black woman as "mule of de world," eloquently address the complexities of Black women's existence. Unlike the women in Hurston's novel, however, these women are ultimately triumphant.

At times in the novel, an embedded narrative apparently developed to support the dominant theme is related to the feminine issue. For example, the schoolteacher Geraldine can be seen simply as a middle-class Black woman who has divorced herself from "real" Afro-American culture. My view, however, is that she is far more complex. What strikes one first is her background: "They [women like Geraldine] come from Mobile. Aiken. From Newport News. From Marietta. From Meridian." These are southern or borderline provincial towns, not quite rural yet not quite urban, in which certain constraints are imposed on social conduct, particularly that of women. "Respectability," an instrument of repression, dictates standards of morality and ethics. Moreover, Geraldine is a product of a Black land-grant college—in the novel's historical period Blacks could not have attended white institutions of higher learning in the South—that primarily serves Black working-class families and allows them entry into the lower middle class, largely as teachers, social workers, and similar professionals.

If we consider these references to town and college, we can

begin to grasp Geraldine's struggle. Here is a woman for whom the immediate environment and the external order have suppressed desire. The college most radically achieves this end:[14]

They go to land-grant colleges, normal schools, and learn how to do the white man's work with refinement: home economics to prepare his food; teacher education to instruct black children in obedience; music to soothe the weary master and entertain his blunted soul. Here they learn the rest of the lesson begun in those soft houses with porch swings and pots of bleeding hearts: how to behave. The careful development of thrift, patience, high morals, and good manners. In short how to get rid of the funkiness. The dreadful funkiness of passion, the funkiness of nature, and the funkiness of a wide range of human emotions. (P. 68)

Funkiness here signifies not merely some primal Afro-American essence but the feminine ("nature," "passion," and "human emotions"). These traits are encoded in our society as within the domain of the feminine, and represent what is being repressed. While the control of passions is the dominant issue, stability and security are corollary concerns. These issues emerge in contrasting portraits of Geraldine's family life and her perception of Pecola's life. The narrator presents Geraldine's life as a symbol of stability:

[Women such as she] never seem to have boyfriends, but they always marry. Certain men watch them, without seeming to, and know that if such a girl is in his house, he will sleep on sheets boiled white, hung out to dry on juniper bushes, and pressed with a heavy iron. There will be pretty paper flowers decorating the picture of his mother, a large Bible in the front room. *They feel secure.* They know their work clothes will be mended, washed, and ironed on Monday, that their Sunday shirts will billow on hangers from the door jamb, stiffly starched and white. They look at her hands and know what she will do with biscuit dough; they smell the coffee and the fried ham; see the white, smoky grits with a dollop of butter on top. Her hips assure them that she will bear children easily and painlessly. And they are right. (Pp. 68–69; Italics added)

What is striking in this passage is its narrative perspective and the objects described. The Bible, the "sheets boiled white," and the mother-in-law's photograph enshrined by flowers have limited use value but have a powerful symbolic force. It would seem limiting, if not wrong, to equate these objects with "bourgeois" values. What they signify is a sense of order and stability; they are, in fact, the symbolic encoding of the myth of respectability. While Geraldine as a type of woman is the apparent focus of the text, the narrator views her life from the aspect of males ("certain men"), and so what is presented is a male perception of such women, a perception shared by the narrator.

The woman is thus erased from the text, or is alternately present and absent. This complicated strategy of representing Geraldine's way of life suggests the social suppression of women such as Geraldine. Their significance is determined solely through their relationship to men. In this context, the denial of sex, the suppression of the erotic, assumes great significance. This denial is empowering for women such as Geraldine.

To Geraldine, Pecola represents not so much an "authentic" aspect of Black life as a force for disorder. She represents all the values that Geraldine has been advised to struggle against:

[Geraldine] looked at Pecola. Saw the dirty, torn dress, the plaits sticking out on her head, hair matted where the plaits had come undone, the muddy shoes with the wad of gum peeping out from beneath the cheap soles, the soiled socks, one of which had been walked down into the shoe. She saw the safety pin holding the hem of the dress up. . . . She had seen this little girl all of her life. Hanging out of windows over saloons in Mobile, crawling over the porches of shotgun houses on the edge of town, sitting in bus stations holding paper bags and crying to mothers who kept saying "Shet up!" Hair uncombed, dresses falling apart, shoes untied and caked with dirt. They had stared at her with great uncomprehending eyes. Eyes that questioned nothing and asked everything. Unblinking and unabashed, they stared up at her. The end of the world lay in their eyes and the beginning and all the waste in heaven. (P. 75)

The description continues with lengthy reflections on the general behavior of the Black underclass that Pecola represents. Far more complex than class, the opposition between the woman and the child is largely inscribed within the terms of order and disorder. Pecola's life is characterized by a "funkiness" that rejects control, ironically the same control that imprisons Geraldine.

In Pauline Breedlove's personal story, the novel fuses narration with an extensive use of the interior monologue. What is presented is a factual, seemingly objective rendering of Pauline's life, elaborated on and reinforced by the interior monologue, which allows the reader to experience Pauline's consciousness of her situation. While the mode of presentation is largely fragmentary, one can link the individual episodes as the monologue comments on Pauline's specific plight as woman, particularly as a Black woman.

Her "fantasies about men and love and touching" are an idealized perception of romantic love. The introduction of males in her life are viewed as a moment of triumph:

In none of her fantasies was she ever aggressive; she was usually idling by the river bank, or gathering berries in a field, when a someone appeared with gentle and penetrating eyes, who—with no exchange of words—understood; and before whose glance her foot straightened and her eyes dropped. The someone had no face, no form, no voice, no order. He was a simple Presence, an all-embracing tenderness with strength and a promise of rest. It did not matter that she had no idea what to do or say to the Presence—after the wordless knowing and the soundless touching, her dreams disintegrated. But the Presence would know what to do. She had only to lay her head on his chest, and he would lead her away to the sea, to the city, to the woods . . . forever. (P. 90)

Here the narrator's voice is fused with Pauline's perception. The passage is consciously literary. The deliberate rhythmic structuring of the sentences and the elaborate use of figurative constructions ("the Presence," "wordless knowing," "soundless touching") identify the language as that of the nar-

rator. Yet the perceptions are clearly Pauline's. Pauline's recognition of Cholly Breedlove as the promised Stranger assumes
a different mode of discourse:

*When I first seed Cholly, I want you to know it was like all the bits of
color from that time down home when all us chil'ren went berry picking
after a funeral and I put some in the pocket of my Sunday dress, and they
mashed up and stained by hips. My whole dress was messed with purple,
and it never did wash out. Not the dress nor me. I could feel that purple
deep inside me. And that lemonade Mama use to make when Pap came
in out of the fields. It be cool and yellowish, with seeds floating near the
bottom. And the streak of green them june bugs made on the trees the night
we left from down home. All them colors was in me. Just sitting there. So
when Cholly came up and tickled my foot, it was like them berries, that
lemonade, them streaks of green the june bugs made, all come together.
Cholly was thin then, with real light eyes. He used to whistle, and when I
heard him, shivers come on my skin. (P. 92)*

The two passages cancel one another and advance an ideology that undermines the notion of romantic love. That concept is undermined by the hyperbolic expressions—the male
as Presence, salvation, redemption—and the description of
the woman as passive. Pauline's simple, earthy response be-
speaks reality. What is stressed are Pauline's innocence and
self-deception. The chaos that later pervades the marriage has
to be viewed within that context.

In interior monologues, Pauline continues to address the
complexity of her plight as a Black woman. Her lowly status is
brought home to her when her employer, Mrs. Foster, advises
her to leave Cholly because of his abusive treatment of her:

*She said she would let me stay if I left him. I thought about that. But
later on it didn't seem none too bright for a black woman to leave a black
man for a white woman. She didn't never give me the eleven dollars she
owed me, neither. That hurt bad. The gas man had cut the gas off, and I
couldn't cook none. . . . She was mad as a wet hen. Kept on telling me
I owed her for uniforms and some old broken down bed she give me. I
didn't know if I owed her or not, but I needed my money. She wouldn't
let up none, neither, even when I give her my word that Cholly wouldn't*

come back there no more. Then I got so desperate I asked her if she would loan it to me. She was quiet for a spell, and then she told me I shouldn't let a man take advantage over me. That I should have more respect, and it was my husband's duty to pay the bills, and if he couldn't, I should leave and get alimony. What was he gone give me alimony on? I seen she didn't understand that all I needed from her was my eleven dollars to pay the gas man so I could cook. (Pp. 95–96)

This episode addresses one of the major areas of conflict between Black women and white women. Pauline obviously places race above any romanticized concept of sisterhood, yet her involvement with Cholly is essentially destructive. The different worlds of the women—separated by both race and class—come into conflict at this point in the narrative, and if there is any truth in Mrs. Foster's assertions, it is undermined by her exploitation of Pauline. Racial solidarity forces Pauline to remain with her husband and tolerate his abuse, while economic circumstances compel her to continue working for her employer. She articulates this conflict at the conclusion of her monologue:

How you going to answer a woman like that, who don't know what a good man is, and say out of one side of her mouth she's thinking of your future but won't give you your own money so you can buy you something besides baloney to eat? So I said, "No good, ma'am. He ain't no good to me. But just the same, I think I'd best stay on." She got up, and I left. When I got outside, I felt pains in my crotch. I held my legs together so tight trying to make that woman understand. But I reckon now she couldn't understand. She married a man with a slash in his face instead of a mouth. So how could she understand? (P. 96)

This essential understanding of herself as a Black woman is revealed again when Pauline gives birth to Pecola. What strikes her is the difference in treatment that doctors accord to Black women and white women:

What'd they think. That just 'cause I knowed how to have a baby with no fuss that my behind wasn't pulling and aching like theirs? Besides that doctor don't know what he talking about. He must never seed no more

foal. Who say they don't have no pain? Just 'cause she don't cry? 'Cause
she can't say it, they think it ain't there? If they looks in her eyes and see
them eyeballs lolling back, see the sorrowful look, they'd know. (P. 99)

This passage again returns to the question of the Black woman
less valued than the white woman in the eyes of the culture. (The foal image evokes again Hurston's Black woman as
mule.) Moreover, Pauline's comments on childbirth become
a metaphor for her total suffering. Voiceless, inarticulate, she
is assumed not to suffer because those who encounter her see
only the exterior.

Sexuality is the domain of empowerment and enslavement
for Pauline (as it was for Geraldine). Pauline speaks of her
moments of intimacy as providing her with the opportunity to
"feel a power." This is the single context of personal affirmation for her. Yet even this power is diminished, and her retreat
into bad faith is marked by the end of that aspect of her life:

But it ain't like that anymore. Most times he's thrashing away inside me
before I'm woke, and through when I am. The rest of the time I can't even
be next to his stinking drunk self. But I don't care 'bout it no more. My
maker will take care of me. I know He will. I know He will. Besides, it
don't make no difference about this old earth. There is sure to be a glory.
(P. 104)

In *The Bluest Eye* each embedded narrative, then, and
especially those focused on women's stories, intensifies the
problem of feminine desire while developing the dominant
themes of the novel. Issues of women's objectification, oppression, and attempts at autonomy (successful or not) are
presented in an episodic fashion and largely unresolved. Subsumed by the larger mythology and the emphasis on form, they
are dissonant chords that usually remain on the periphery of
the text.

In the male narratives, an equally complex narration occurs. Most males play secondary roles in the novel, their stories
unfolding largely within the narratives of women. Men in general are presented as hostile to women, the lone exception

being Mister MacTeer, whose characterization is subordinate to that of Mrs. MacTeer. Yet the larger text offers contradictory constructions of male characters. They must be seen as agents in the larger myth and at the same time as flawed creatures.

The narrative achieves this end through its use of irony, often resulting in the transmission of conflicting messages. Linda Hutcheon addresses the significance of irony in her study of parody as an artistic device:

The pragmatic function of irony . . . is one of signalling evaluation, most frequently of a pejorative nature. Its mockery can, but need not, take the usual form of laudatory expressions employed to imply a negative judgment; on the semantic level, this involves the deployment of manifest praise to hide mocking blame. . . . Irony functions, therefore, as both antiphrasis and an evaluative strategy that implies an attitude of encoding agents towards the text itself, an attitude which, in turn, allows and demands the decoder's interpretation and evaluation.[15]

In *The Bluest Eye*, this use of irony is dramatically revealed in the characterization of Cholly Breedlove. His story reinforces the major myths of the novel. He is depicted as having been abandoned by his father, rejected by his mother, and humiliated in his sexual initiation by white males. Each detail of his life invites the reader to sympathize with Cholly and forgive his rape of Pecola. The reader is further seduced into this response by the narrator's seeming romanticizing of Cholly's life:

The pieces of Cholly's life could become coherent only in the head of a musician. Only those who talk their talk through the gold of curved metal, or in the touch of the black-and-white rectangles and taut skins and strings echoing from wooden corridors, could give form to this life. . . . Only a musician would sense, know, without even knowing that he knew that Cholly was free. Dangerously free. Free to feel whatever he felt—fear, guilt, shame, love, grief, pity. Free to be tender or violent, to whistle or weep. Free to sleep in doorways or between the white sheets of a singing woman. Free to take a job, free to leave it. . . . Free to take a woman's insults, for his body had already conquered hers. Free to be gentle when she was sick, or mop her floor, for she knew what and where his maleness was. . . . He was free to live his fantasies, and free even to die, the how and the when of which held no interest to him. In those days, Cholly was truly free. Abandoned in a junk heap by his mother, rejected for a crap game by his father, there was nothing more to lose. He was alone with his own perceptions and appetites. (Pp. 125–126)

This description of Cholly's life leads the reader to view his brutal treatment of Polly, as well as his rape of Pecola, as acts ultimately generated by a brutal system of dehuminization. The implicit argument is that social forces have conspired to produce the kind of man represented by Cholly—an argument consistent with one of the major themes of the novel. Yet a close reading of the rape scene raises other issues. The narration of the incident from Cholly's viewpoint rather than that of Pecola permits an apparent sympathetic treatment of him. Yet key passages from the episode reveal recurrent moments of textual dissonance. After "stagger[ing] home reeling drunk," Cholly experiences several conflicting responses to his daughter. His first response is structured by fantasies of violence and pity:

The clear statement of her misery was an accusation. He wanted to break her neck—but tenderly. Guilt and impotence rose in a bilious duet. What could he do for her—ever? What give her? What could a burned-out black man say to the hunched back of his eleven-year-old daughter? If he looked into her face, he would see those haunted, loving eyes. . . . How dare she love him? Hadn't she any sense at all? (P. 127)

The moment of sexual arousal is still couched within a context of tenderness. Recalling a previous erotic moment with Pauline, he approaches the rape of his daughter:

The tenderness welled up in him, and he sank to his knees, his eyes on the foot of his daughter. Crawling on all fours toward her, he raised his hand and caught the foot in an awkward stroke. Cholly raised his other hand to her hips to save her from falling. He put his head down and nibbled at the back of her leg. His mouth trembled at the firm sweetness of the flesh. He closed his eyes, letting his fingers dig into her waist. The rigidness of her shocked body, the silence of her stunned throat, was better than Pauline's easy laughter had been. . . . He wanted to fuck her—tenderly. But the tenderness would not hold. The tightness of her vagina was more than he could bear. His soul seemed to slip down into his guts and fly out into her, and the gigantic thrust he made into her then provoked the only sound she made—a hollow suck of air in the back of her throat. Like the rapid loss of air from a circus balloon. (P. 128)

While the narrative focuses on the rapist rather than the victim, what becomes clear in the passage is a textual deconstruction in which the description becomes an ironic one. Central to this strategy is the recurrent use of *tender* and *tenderness* in a context that is clearly intended to be ironic. Cholly envisions "tenderly" breaking his daughter's neck, fantasizes about violating her body with "tenderness," and wants to "fuck" her "tenderly." At one level, what is presented is free indirect discourse in which the text provides a dual voice; the narrator's and character's perspectives are merged so that there is an interweaving of the two positions. The oxymoronic construction itself undermines whatever sympathies one has for Cholly. The fusion of tenderness with acts of fantasized and real violence is experienced by the reader as a contradiction. Consequently, Cholly's antiheroic stature is significantly diminished in the text. This is reinforced at the end of the description, when the narrative focus shifts to Pecola: "So when the child regained consciousness, she was lying on the kitchen floor under a heavy quilt, trying to connect the pain between her legs with the face of her mother looming over her" (P. 129).

Soaphead Church is another character who is presented ironically in the novel. His presence is needed by the narrative progression—someone has to provide blue eyes for Pecola—and his character contributes to the overall fictional construction of a Black community. He represents those faith healers

who prey on the less educated and superstitious in the community. Imbued with a mystical aura, he assumes mystical
proportions. Even the opening lines of his narrative suggests
the otherworldly: "Once there was an old man. . . ." And in
his personal narrative of color, caste, and class, the context
for understanding his character is provided. The same ironic
strategy used in describing Cholly's rape of his daughter is employed in the narrator's description of Soaphead's pedophilia:

He could have been an active homosexual but lacked the courage.
Bestiality did not occur to him, and sodomy was quite out of the
question, for he did not experience sustained erections and could
not endure the thought of somebody else's. . . . He abhorred flesh
on flesh. The sight of dried matter in the corner of the eye, decayed
or missing teeth, ear wax, blackheads, moles, blisters, skin crusts—
all the natural excretions and protections the body was capable of—
disquieted him. His attentions therefore gradually settled on those
humans whose bodies were least offensive—children. And since he
was too diffident to confront homosexuality, and since little boys
were insulting, scary, and stubborn, he further limited his interest
to little girls. They were usually manageable and frequently seduc-
tive. His sexuality was anything but lewd; his patronage of little girls
smacked of innocence and was associated in his mind with cleanli-
ness. He was what one might call a very clean old man. (P. 132)

The details provided are subverted by the last sentence of the
text. To view Soaphead as "a very clean old man," after depicting his manipulation of children, and especially his exploitation of the weakness and innocence of little girls, is to alter
his position radically. Soaphead further satirizes his position
when he describes his conduct in a "letter" to God:

The little girls are the only things I'll miss. Do you know that when
I touched their sturdy little tits and bit them—just a little—I felt
I was being friendly? I didn't want to kiss their mouths or sleep in
the bed with them or take a child bride for my own. Playful, I felt,
and friendly. Not like the newspapers said. Not like the people whispered. And they didn't mind at all. Not at all. Remember how so

many of them came back? No one would even try to understand that.
. . . With little girls it is all clean and good and friendly. (P. 143)

Sula

Critical readings of *Sula* have focused on the novel's extensive treatment of the relationship between Sula and Nel, a relationship generally assumed to reveal the work's specific feminist dimension. Yet closer readings show that the Sula–Nel relationship, although one of the novel's dominant themes, is contained within a larger textual enterprise. Moreover, that larger enterprise determines the relationship and is the dominant focus of the novel.

Central to *Sula* is the construction of myth, and through its strategies of narration, the form of the novel becomes dominant. The attention to minor details to effect the real, the graphic descriptions of individual acts, the detailed incorporation of folklore—all constitute the larger theme in which the Sula–Nel narrative is enclosed. The reader is immediately placed in this world in the ironic naming of the Black section of Medallion:

A joke. A nigger joke. That was the way it got started. Not the town, of course, but that part of town where the Negroes lived, the part they called the Bottom in spite of the fact that it was up in the hills. Just a nigger joke. The kind white folks tell when the mill closes down and they're looking for a little comfort somewhere. The kind colored folks tell on themselves when the rain doesn't come for weeks, and they're looking for a little comfort somehow.[16]

The narrator completes the history of the Bottom by relating how "the master," through guile, swindled "the slave" of a valuable piece of land. The town, then, assumes not only a personal history but becomes a metaphor for the kinds of relationships historically existing between Blacks and whites. Most important, it functions as a frame, in much the same manner as the marigolds do in *The Bluest Eye*. At the conclusion of the novel, the focus returns to the Bottom, noting the changes that have occurred there over forty years and the displacement of its Black population. The narrative of the town becomes the frame that encloses and subordinates all other narratives. First and foremost, the novel is the story of the town.

The personal history of Helene Wright, the construction of the Peace family, the presentation of Shadrack and his National Suicide Day, the deweys—they are all part of a larger picture that elaborates on the character of the town. Each episode, each individual representation, is significant primarily because it illuminates the character of the Bottom.

Such an enterprise becomes a containment strategy in the narrative. One major effect of this is that the complexities of women's issues, although suggested in the text, are often passed over or presented elliptically. For example, the reader is provided with a somewhat fragmentary sketch of the background of Helene Wright and must construct a narrative of his or her own to flesh out the spaces. Helene is presented as a descendant of New Orleans Creoles who struggles to retain her past and yet tries to reject it. She accomplishes this by her emphasis on propriety and perfection.

Helene Wright was an impressive woman, at least in Medallion she was. Heavy hair in a bun, dark eyes arched in a perpetual query about other people's manners. A woman who won all social battles with presence and conviction of the legitimacy of her authority. Since there was no Catholic church in Medallion then, she joined the most conservative black church. And held sway. It was Helene who never turned her head in church when latecomers arrived; Helene who established the practice of seasonal altar flowers; Helene who introduced the giving of banquets of welcome to returning Negro veterans. She lost only one battle—the pronunciation of her name. The people in the Bottom refused to say Helene. They called her Helen Wright and left it at that. (P. 18)

Helene's narrative is marked by constant references to her inauthenticity. Her deferential treatment of the white train conductor earns her the scorn of the Black soldiers on the train as well as that of her own daughter. Her attempt to stifle any signs of life in Nel reinforces the image of inauthenticity. Yet the omissions from her narrative allow the reader to experience her as a far more complex character. Even in the name "Creole" there is a confusion of identity. What Helene represents are the mulattas and quadroons who are both rejected and accepted by Blacks and whites. As a "daughter of a Creole whore," she is constantly aware of her vulnerability. At one point, the narrative digresses to allude to that situation:

It was November, November 1920. Even in Medallion there was a victorious swagger in the legs of white men and a dull-eyed excitement in the eyes of colored veterans.

Helene thought about the trip South with heavy misgiving but decided that she had the best protection: her manner and her bearing, to which she would add a beautiful dress. She bought some deep-brown wool and three-fourths of a yard of matching velvet. Out of this she made herself a heavy but elegant dress with velvet collar and pockets. (P. 19)

What is striking here is the introduction of a specific sexual threat, a threat for which the text does not prepare the reader. These sexual tensions and ambivalences are played out on the train ride, but their broader historical significance is not developed.

Another manner in which the feminine is introduced is through the characterization of the Peace women. They are totally free in their expressions of sexuality and economic autonomy. These women operate outside the norms of their community, for which they are both celebrated and questioned. Hannah, who "would practically fuck anything," is shown in the following light:

Hannah exasperated the women in the town—the "good" women, who said, "One thing I can't stand is a nasty woman"; the whores who were hard put to find trade among black men anyway and who resented Hannah's generosity; the middling women, who had both husbands and affairs, because Hannah seemed too unlike them, having no passion attached to her relationships and being wholly incapable of jealousy. Hannah's friendships with women were, of course, seldom and short-lived, and the newly married couples whom her mother took in soon learned what a hazard she was. She could break up a marriage before it had even become one—she would make love to the new groom and wash his wife's dishes all in an afternoon. What she wanted after Rekus died, and what she succeeded in having more often than not, was some touching everyday.

The men, surprisingly, never gossiped about her. She was unquestionably a kind and generous woman and that, coupled with her extraordinary beauty and funky elegance of manner, made them defend her and protect her from the vitriol that newcomers or their wives might spill. (Pp. 44–45)

The shift in narrative away from Hannah as agent to the town's response to her conduct undermines the characterization of her as a strong person. What emerges from this portrait is an independent woman motivated by her own insecurity ("What she wanted . . . was some touching everyday") who has been excluded from all the communities of women and left solely with the male population to defend her. Her burning to death seems no more than an elaboration of the myth, and the issues generated by her independence remain open.

This ambivalent treatment of women's independence and autonomy is even more dramatically played out in the representations of Nel and Sula. The reader's initial introduction to them suggests two characters in rebellion:

So when they met, first in those chocolate halls and next through the ropes of the swing, they felt the ease and comfort of old friends. Because each had discovered years before that they were neither white nor male, and that all freedom and triumph was forbidden to them, they set about creating something else to be. Their meeting was fortunate, for it let them use each other to grow on. Daughters of distant mothers and incomprehensible fathers (Sula's because he was dead; Nel's because he wasn't), they found in each other's eyes the intimacy they were looking for. (P. 53)

But this awareness of their historical roles in terms of race and gender is summarily dismissed early in the narrative. The reader is led to believe that Nel's submission to Jude could be explained by her parents' stifling of her imagination. Yet it barely explains the intensity of her response:

Nel's response to Jude's shame and anger selected her away from Sula. And greater than her friendship was this new feeling of being needed by someone who saw her singly. She didn't even know she had a neck until Jude remarked on it, or that her smile was anything but the spreading of her lips until he saw it as a small miracle. (P. 84)

The major thrust of this description is that Nel, presented earlier as a rebel who cast her lot with Sula, is seen as not merely passively accepting the conventional role of bride but actually rejoicing in it. While the conclusion of the novel indicates a moment in which Nel suddenly realizes that it was her separation from Sula that caused her pain, there is no sense in which that insight even remotely enters her mind earlier.

Through this narrative strategy, a significant period of Sula's personal history is glossed over. Her ten-year absence is referred to by a single sentence at the end of the first section of the novel: "It would be ten years before [Sula and Nel] saw each other again, and their meeting would be thick with birds" (p. 85). Yet it is apparent that during that time, Sula has undergone significant personal changes and returns to Medallion as a rebel. The mystery is heightened by a conversation between Nel and Sula in which Nel attempts to learn more about Sula's life away from Medallion:

"Tell me about it. The big city."
"Big is all it is. A big Medallion."
"No. I mean the life. The nightclubs, and parties . . ."
"I was in college, Nellie. No nightclubs on campus."
"Campus? That's what they call it? Well, you wasn't in no college for—what—ten years now? And you didn't write to nobody. How come you never wrote?" (P. 99)

This suppression of an essential period in Sula's history keeps the novel focused on the town. Just the opposite occurs in the novel's portrayal of Shadrack's war experience, which also takes place outside Medallion and is presented in the opening scenes of the novel, thereby providing a context for his behavior. With Sula, however, all background is omitted from the text, and we view her behavior largely as it is mediated by the town and the narrator.

Sula's return, therefore, is placed within the pattern of beliefs in the town. The passages that provide the frame for her return focus exclusively on the epistemology that governs the town. Particularly reinforced is the townpeople's approach to confronting evil, death, nature, and their position as an oppressed people:

> What was taken by outsiders to be slackness, slovenliness, or even generosity was in fact a full recognition of the legitimacy of forces other than good ones. They did not believe doctors could heal—for them, none ever had done so. They did not believe death was accidental—life might be, but death was deliberate. They did not believe that Nature was ever askew—only inconvenient. Plague and drought were as "natural" as springtime. If milk could curdle, God knows robins could fall. The purpose of evil was to survive it and they determined (without ever knowing they had made up their minds to do it) to survive floods, white people, tuberculosis, famine and ignorance. They knew anger well but not despair, and they didn't stone sinners for the same reason they didn't commit suicide—it was beneath them. (P. 90)

What is dominant, then, is the construction of the Bottom as a repository of Black culture. Yet interspersed throughout this characterization is a subtext that addresses Sula's rebellion. Her confrontation with Eva, especially Sula's rejection of the conventional roles of marriage and motherhood, strongly supports this. Even more significant is her description of Black male culture:

> I mean, I don't know what the fuss is about. I mean, everything in the world loves you. White men love you. They spend so much time worrying about your penis, they forget their own. The only thing they want to do is to cut off a nigger's privates. And if that ain't love and respect I don't know what is. And white women? They chase

you all to every corner of the earth, feel for you under every bed. . . . Colored women worry themselves into just trying to hang on to your cuffs. Even little children . . . spend all their childhood eating their hearts out 'cause they think you don't love them. And if that ain't enough, you love yourselves. Nothing in this world loves a black man more than another black man. (P. 104)

Such moments of rebellion, however, largely remain fragmented and elliptical. Having no context, they appear as givens, and the reader must construct a text that will illuminate them. The dominant focus remains on the Bottom, and Sula's character is viewed only as it is filtered through the minds of the townspeople. The narrator's representation of their rejection of Sula over a significant social transgression clearly illustrates this narrative strategy:

But it was the men who gave her the final label, who fingerprinted her for all time. . . . They said that Sula slept with white men. *It may not have been true, but it certainly could have been. She was obviously capable of it.* In any case, all minds were closed to her when the word was passed around. It made the old women draw their lips together; made small children look away from her in shame; made young men fantasize elaborate torture for her—just to get the saliva back in their mouths when they saw her. (Pp. 112–113; italics added)

With the exception of the italicized portion of the passage, the focus is on the reaction of the town. Yet the act itself, if indeed it did occur, would constitute a significant act of rebellion by Sula. Her position, however, is left indeterminate and remains largely subordinate to the larger purpose of representing the town. Sula as character merely becomes another vehicle for the exploration of other issues.

This shift in narrative focus often undermines Sula's freedom in the text. The most dramatic example is the episode that follows the sexual encounter between Jude and Sula. Moreover, the narrative angle after the adulterous scene between Sula and Jude is designed to gain sympathy for Nel. The fusion of indirect discourse and interior monologue is designed to generate pathos:

Could he be gone if his tie is still here? He will remember it and come back and then she would . . . uh. Then she could . . . tell him. Sit down quietly and tell him. "But Jude," she would say, "you *knew* me. My ways and my hands and how my stomach folded and how we tried to get Mickey to nurse and how about that time when the landlord said . . . but you said . . . and I cried, Jude. You knew me and had listened to the things I said in the night and heard me in the bathroom and laughed at my raggedy girdle and I laughed too because I knew you too, Jude. So how could you leave me when you knew me?" (Pp. 104–105)

The focus on Nel's response clearly takes away whatever sympathy the reader might be inclined to feel for Sula. The emotionally devastating impact that the act had on Nel renders the issue of Sula's freedom secondary. Much of this is reinforced in the encounter between Nel and Sula as Sula lies dying:

> "You can't have it all, Sula. 'Specially if you don't want people to have to do for you."
>
> "Neither one, Nellie. Neither one."
>
> "You can't have it all, Sula." Nel was getting exasperated with her lying at death's door still smart-talking.
>
> "Why? I can do it all, why can't I have it all?"
>
> "You *can't* do it all. You a woman and a colored woman at that. You can't act like a man. You can't be walking around all independent-like, doing whatever you like, taking what you want, leaving what you don't."
>
> "You repeating yourself."
>
> "How repeating myself?"
>
> "You say I'm a woman and colored. Ain't that the same as being a man?" (P. 142)

A crucial issue is left largely unresolved in the text. Sula's final query to Nel about how would either one of them know who was good leaves the issue open ("I mean maybe it wasn't you. Maybe it was me."). What is clear is that the independent woman dies removed from her community and unreconciled with her friend. If the text does not totally reject this notion of independence, it subordinates it to other issues.

The Bluest Eye and *Sula*, then, are narratives marked by tensions and dissonances generated by contending discourses. The primary focuses—the production of "literariness" and the semiotic and mythological construction of a Black "village" or community—are disrupted by the insertion of feminine desire, which takes the form of embedded narratives that relate stories of the oppression of women, ambivalent and ironic characterizations and representations of males, and shifts in narrative perspective that allow specific mediations by the external narrator.

FOUR

♦

Desire, Ambivalence, and Nationalist–Feminist Discourse in Bambara's Short Stories

THE SEVERAL WAYS in which Toni Cade Bambara's short stories were produced assured them a wide audience. Collected and presented as single texts, they were widely anthologized in feminist anthologies, particularly those produced by "women of color";[1] and Bambara often read them aloud as "performance pieces" before audiences. Yet they have rarely been the object of in-depth critical attention.[2]

Bambara's role as storyteller resembles Walter Benjamin's description of such a person. Benjamin's storyteller, a person "always rooted in the people," creates a narrative largely grounded in the oral tradition of his or her culture and containing something useful in the way of a moral, proverb, or maxim that audiences can integrate into their experiences and share with others. Hence, the story becomes the medium through which groups of people are unified, values sustained, and a shared world view sedimented.[3]

Benjamin's reflections on the story in general are relevant to the cultural practices that informed the production of the Afro-American short story, which is largely rooted in the Black oral tradition. Many Afro-American writers, among them Hurston, Chesnutt, Ellison, and Wright, not only produced short stories but incorporated into their novels folklore drawn from the oral culture.

Working within this framework, Bambara attaches political significance to the short story. Introducing an early collection of her short stories for Black children, she discusses the historical link between Afro-American folktales and short stories. She creates for her readers an imagined setting in which Black families gathered in kitchens to share stories that challenged and corrected representations of Blacks in the dominant historical discourse, fiction, and film. She urges young readers to "be proud of our oral tradition, our elders who tell their tales in the kitchen. For they are truth." In an interview with Claudia Tate, Bambara elaborated on her commitment to the short story, stating that she viewed it as highly effective for establishing political dialogue:

I prefer the short story genre because it's quick, it makes a modest appeal for attention, it can creep up on you on your blind side. The reader comes to the short story with a mindset different than that which he approaches the big book, and a different set of controls operating, which is why I think the short story is far more effective in terms of teaching us lessons.[4]

Like her works in other genres, Bambara's short stories primarily aim at truth speaking, particularly as *truth* is related to the semiotic mediation of Black existential modalities. Of primary importance are the construction and representation of an organic Black community and the articulation of Black nationalist ideology. Nevertheless, her two short story collections, *Gorilla, My Love* and *The Seabirds Are Still Alive*, are marked by dissonance and ruptures; in both volumes, Bambara's insertion of themes related to the desires of Black women and girls disrupts and often preempts the stories' primary focus on classic realism and nationalism.

In *Gorilla*, Bambara's use of the young girl Hazel as the primary narrator results in a decentering of the stories. In each narrative, a subtext focused on issues with which girls and women are confronted threatens to displace the racial discourse that is in the dominant text. The stories in *Seabirds*, which are generally more explicitly political than those in *Gorilla*, directly inscribe the tensions between racial and gender politics. The stories in *Seabirds*, then, signal a pre-emergent feminist consciousness. In this collection, more complex development and representations of Black women of "the community," increased marginalization and deconstruction of mythologies centered on Black males, and the general highlighting of feminine and feminist issues indicate a heightening of tensions between gender and racial politics.

Gorilla, My Love

Published as individual stories over a twelve-year period from 1959 to 1972, and issued as a single volume in 1972, *Gorilla, My Love* marked Bambara's debut as a spokesperson for Black cultural nationalism. The stories in this volume were generally received as innocent children's narratives that presented realistic depictions of an organic Black community. Focusing on neighborhoods of ordinary Black working-class people, they ignored larger global issues of their time—racial strife in urban areas, the Vietnam involvement, political assassinations, and independence struggles in Africa—and dealt exclusively with the "inner world" of Blacks.[5]

The stories in *Gorilla* clearly locate the collection in the broad context of Black nationalist fiction of the 1960s. Employing classic realism as their dominant narrative form, Bambara constructed organic Black communities in which intraracial strife was minimal, the White world remained on the periphery, and the pervasive "realities" of Black life were presented. Their model readers were those who were acquainted with nationalist semiotic representations of the Black communities of the 1960s.

Throughout the stories, however, submerged narratives, or subtexts, address the desires of Black women, moving away from the focus on classic realism and nationalist ideology. A close examination of *Gorilla*'s narrative perspective reveals a disruption of the text's apparent unity in the construction of Black female subjects and representation of Black males, particularly the displacing and demythologizing of legendary and heroic Black figures.

The privileged position of the narrator in *Gorilla* is reinforced by Hazel, the young Black girl, who is the first-person narrator of most of the stories in the collection. Her authenticity is underlined by her total cultural identification with the community she describes. With her mastery of the restricted linguistic code of Black urban life and her ability to evoke both the verbal and nonverbal signs of that culture, she speaks from within that world and becomes a self-ethnographer of the imaginary Black community. For readers familiar with the culture, Hazel provides a body of signs that resonate with their semiotic comprehension of the culture; for readers unfamiliar with the culture, she offers "realistic" insights. This process of narration can be understood in Werner Sollors's discussion of James Weldon Johnson's concept of the "problem of the double audience" for Black writers. Applying Johnson's concept to "ethnic writers in general," Sollors argues that such writers "confront an actual imagined double audience composed of 'insiders' and of readers, listeners, or spectators who are not familiar with the writer's ethnic group [functioning as] translators of ethnicity to ignorant, and sometimes hostile outsiders and, at the same time as mediators between 'America' and greenhorns."[6]

An episode in the title story of the collection dramatically illustrates the narrative strategy. Commenting on the manner in which her mother confronts teachers when Hazel encounters difficulties, the child reflects:

My momma come up there in a minute when them teachers start playin the dozens behind colored folks. She stalk in with her hat pulled down bad and that Persian lamb coat draped back over one hip on account of she got her fist planted there so she can talk that talk which gets us all hypnotized, and the teacher be comin undone cause she know this would be her job and her behind cause Momma got pull with the board and bad by her own self anyhow.[7]

What is striking here is the exclusive deployment of an alternative code, one that attempts to reproduce the nuances of Black urban speech and diverges significantly from the linguistic forms of the dominant culture; at the same time, however, the substance is accessible to those familiar with the culture and to those who are not. References to the cultural practices of Black life, all grounded in specific semiotic structures, evoke for the reader familiar with that culture a recognizable world and transmit "realistic" information to those outside it. The references to playing the dozens, semantic constructions such as "talk that talk" and "be comin undone," the use of the term "bad" as a synonym for good, and the mother's physical statement as a semiotics of the body[8] all contribute to the symbolic construction of a Black community and emphasize Hazel's role as that of an authentic self-ethnographer. Moreover, the first-person narration, particularly within the context of an alternative code, places the speaker in an authoritative position. As William Riggan points out:

First person narration carries with it an inherent quality of realism and conviction based on a claim to firsthand experience and knowledge. The very fact that we have before us, either literally or figuratively, an identifiable narrator telling us the story directly, even metaphorically grabbing us on the arm, gesturing to us individually or collectively from time to time, imparts a tangible reality to the narrative situation and a substantial veracity to the account we are reading or "hearing."[9]

Hazel's role as narrator, then, particularly her use of a linguistic code that is largely a reproduction of Black working-class speech, allows her to construct authoritatively the implied imaginary community, block, or neighborhood. Recognition of the inner world of that community by readers is thereby contingent on their acceptance of Hazel's credibility and their ability to decode the body of signs evoked in the story. Moreover, Bambara's narrative strategy of using a young girl to tell a story about an older Black woman allows her to develop a feminine dimension that situates the narrative in race- and gender-specific contexts.

Gorilla draws on oral cultural practices that are rather commonplace in Afro-American literature; "The Johnson Girls" makes a more radical use of such practices. In this story, Hazel mediates a lively exchange in which three women offer their views about men:

"First you gotta have you a fuckin man, a cat that can get down between the sheets without a whole lotta bullshit about "This is a spiritual union" or "Women are always rippin off my body. . . ."

"Amen," say Marcy.

"Course, he usually look like hell and got no I.Q. atall," say Sugar.

"So you gots to have you a go-around man, a dude that can put in a good appearance so you won't be shame to take him round your friends, case he insists on opening his big mouth."

"Course, the go-around man ain't about you, he got his rap and his wardrobe and his imported deodorant stick with the foreign ingredients listed there at the bottom in some unknown tongue. Which means you gots to have a gofor." (P. 168)

The reproduction of the rhythms and cadences of oral cultural practices links this passage to the urban Black subculture. It is also linked to oral and performance texts of Afro-American culture by the verbal exchanges between the women, which reproduce the chant–response ritual characteristic of similar exchanges between fundamentalist ministers and their congregations. Bambara appropriates "signifying," the somewhat crude banter that occurs between Blacks (usually men and boys) in working-class Afro-American communities. Central to this practice is the use of hyperbolic and scatological tropes as strategies for criticizing and disparaging an opponent.[10] Traditionally, these cultural practices were the domain of Black male speakers and writers, and they are usually associated with the construction of the myth of the Black male as competitive, assertive, and combative.[11] Bambara's story, then, signals an appropriation and retextualization.

Bambara relies on signifying for its traditional function: to mark the text as race specific and to conflate the oral and written modes of textual production. Bambara's use of signifying, particularly her identification of the practice with women, is an important part of a complex strategy. Laurent Jenny provides a useful theoretical tool for examining Bambara's textual strategies in his distinction between "weak" strategies (i.e., those that are largely marked by transportation of sign systems from one text to another) and strategies that produce an ideological effect. Arguing for the critical function of the latter, he says:

The author repeats in order to encircle, to enclose within another discourse, thus rendered more powerful. He speaks in order to obliterate, or cancel. Or else, patiently, he gainsays in order to go beyond. . . . Since it is impossible to forget or neutralize the discourse, one might as well subvert its ideological poles; or reify it, make it the object of a metalanguage. Then the possibility of a new parole will open up, growing out of the cracks of the old discourse, rooted in them. In spite of themselves these old discourses will drive all the force they have gained as stereotypes into the *parole* which contradicts them, they will energize it. Intertextuality thus forces them to finance their own subversion.[12]

Bambara's narrative engages in a female appropriation of the signifying practice in order to allow feminine consciousness to assert itself. The narrative is the method by which the speakers inform their readers of women's desires and the perceived deficiencies of men, and it reinforces this epistemological context by presenting it within a traditionally male cultural practice. The myth of the autonomous woman is produced here and is strengthened by the use of chant and response and signifying practices.

Central to the representations of Black adolescent girls

are the traits of rebelliousness, assertiveness, and, at times, physical aggressiveness. Taken collectively, these traits signify a rejection of society's stereotypes of females as fragile and vulnerable and the construction of alternative selves that oppose and negate the ideology that structures the girls' community. In the representation of Hazel, the protagonist whose voice permeates the narratives, autonomy and self-definition are asserted forcefully.

In the title story, Hazel and not her brothers confronts the manager of the theater when the children are cheated; she assumes responsibility for physically protecting her handicapped brother in the story "Raymond's Run"; and she confronts the police officers who interrupt the basketball game that she and Manny are playing. In her rejection of behaviors specifically assigned by the culture to young girls, she directly challenges the ideological assumptions that dictate the role of the Black female "on the block." Hazel's rebellion dominates the text and manifests itself in both her actions and her implicit defiance (e.g., the street jargon and obscenities that mark her speech). Burning a theater that misled the children by misrepresenting its program, being consistently successful in athletic competition, and being able to protect herself and assert her authority on the block all mark her as a tough and independent adolescent girl who successfully rebels against traditional roles.

This toughness and independence are strongly depicted in an episode from "Raymond's Run" in which Hazel, who is walking with her handicapped brother, sees two of her rivals approaching:

So, they are steady coming up Broadway and I see right away that it's going to be one of those Dodge City scenes cause the street ain't that big and they're close to the buildings just as we are. . . . But as they get to me they slow down. I'm ready to fight, cause like I said I don't feature a whole lot of chit chat. I much prefer to just knock you down right from the jump and save everybody a lotta precious time. (P. 25)

The rejection of "approved" feminine roles is made even more explicit in Hazel's refusal to participate in the May Pole dancing. She informs the reader:

You'd think my mother'd be grateful not to have to make me a white organdy dress with a big satin sash and buy me new white baby-doll shoes that she can't be taken out of the box till the big day. You'd think she'd be glad her daughter ain't out there prancing around a May Pole getting the new clothes all dirty and sweaty and trying to act like a fairy or a flower or whatever you're supposed to be when you should be trying to be yourself, whatever that is, which is, as far as I'm concerned, a poor Black girl who really can't afford to buy shoes and a new dress you wear once a lifetime cause it won't fit next year. (P. 27)

Hazel's rebellion against socially dictated roles is further emphasized by her commentary on the hostility that the community encourages between girls and women. Referring to the difficulty she is having in establishing a real friendship with Gretchen, she observes: "Gretchen smiles, but it's not a smile, and I'm thinking girls never really smile at each other because they don't know how and don't want to know how and there's probably no one to teach us how, cause grown-up girls don't know either" (pp. 26–27).

At the end of the race, which she wins while Gretchen finishes second, Hazel returns to this theme of separation:

We stand there with this big smile of respect between us. It's about as real a smile as girls can do for each other, considering we don't practice real smiling every day, you know, cause maybe we too busy being flowers or fairies or strawberries instead of being something honest and worthy of respect. . . . you know . . . like being people. (P. 32)

This apparently innocent "children's story" marks the emergence of a consciousness grounded in feminine and proto-feminist experiences. The questioning and challenging of gender roles, the insertion of the problem of female bonding in the text, and, most significantly, the construction of a rebellious antisocial girl protagonist produce counterdiscourses that challenge the dominant hierarchical discourse of Black cultural nationalism.

In addition to challenging gender-determined roles for girls and women, the stories in *Gorilla* address the plight of young girls as victims of the predatory sexual practices of the community's Black males. In "Sweet Town," the protagonist Kit romanticizes and mystifies the sexual act:

There is a certain glandular disturbance all beautiful, wizardly, great people have second sight to, that trumpet through the clothes, sets the nerves up for the kill, and torments the orange explosure. . . . My mother calls it sex and my brother says it's groin fever time. But then they are always ones for brevity. (P. 122)

Having submitted to B.J., who seduces her by pretending to share her romanticized view of the world, Kit finds herself discarded as he plans to run away with a male friend. Her idealized vision of eroticism and romance is completely shattered when she is forced to recognize the crude opportunism and cynicism that mark a vision that is antithetical to it.

"The Basement" introduces the issue of the sexual molestation of children, strongly emphasizing the vulnerability of Black adolescent girls "on the block" to the sexual desires of older men. The seriousness of the issue is suppressed by the narrative in which Hazel innocently relates the events, highlighting the comic exchanges between the two women identified as "Patsy Aunt" and "Patsy Mother." In a somewhat straightforward manner, Hazel and her friend Patsy are warned not to go into the basement of the building in which the superintendent lives because he "mess[es] with young girls." Discussing this problem with the two girls, Patsy's aunt and mother discover that the superintendent frequently exposes himself to young girls at play, and "Patsy Mother" rushes to the basement to assault him.

The incident is related lightheartedly in the story, but beneath the simplicity and the moments of vulgarity and the raucous laughter, the sexual aggressiveness of men in the community—particularly the manner in which that aggressiveness represents a threat to young girls and women—is addressed as a serious problem. Responding to Hazel's curiosity about the need to stay away from the basement, two older women discuss male sexual aggression:

"Because," said Patsy Aunt drownin [Patsy's mother] out, "some men when they get to drinking don't know how to behave properly to women and girls. Understand?" "You see," said Patsy Mother, back again [from her trip to the basement] and with only one slipper, "it's very hard to teach young girls to be careful and at the same time not to scare you to death. . . . Sex is not a bad thing. But sometimes it's a need that makes men act bad, take advantage of little girls who are friendly and trusting. Understand?" (P. 143)

The incident assumes major significance when it is seen within the context of the repressed and unspoken of the text.[13] Beneath the laughter and flippancy is an alternative narrative that addresses the community as the site of the victimization of women by the aggressive sexual appetites of the males among whom they must live.

Stories that focus on the plight of older women also mark Gorilla's concern with feminine and feminist discourse. These stories address one or more of three themes: (1) the women's need to establish protective bonds with young girls in the community in order to pass on to them advice needed for survival; (2) the necessity of examining and questioning traditional male–female relationships; and (3) the necessity of challenging and rebelling against roles assigned to women in the larger society in general and "on the block" in particular.

The process by which adult women transmit the knowledge necessary for survival is most in evidence in "The Johnson Girls" and "The Basement." These two narratives detail the responsibilities assumed by older Black women in protecting young Black girls from destructive male behavior. Great Ma Drew's observation in "The Johnson Girls" emphasizes that this responsibility is part of a traditional cultural relationship between women and girls; at the time of her childhood, "the older women would gather together to train young girls in the ways of menfolks" (p. 165). In "Maggie of the Green Bottles," the older woman not only verbally transmits folk wisdom to the young girl but actually uses herself as an exemplar of female rebellion and independence. In her defiance of the community's attempts to control the lives of women through intersecting institutions of domination (the Black cultural tradition, the fundamentalist church, and male hegemony), Maggie places herself outside, and in opposition to, her society, thereby creating a free, transcendent self.

Hazel's role as first-person narrator results in the suppression of direct ideological statements, but the spiritual bond between woman and girl is uppermost in the story. Reflecting on her grandmother's life, Hazel suggests that Maggie embrace a view of the world that is not only antithetical to the values of the community but also represents a consciousness that questions that value system and places her outside it:

> I am told by those who knew her . . . that Margaret Cooper Williams wanted something she could not have. And it was the sorrow of her life that all her children and theirs were uncooperative, worse squeamish. Too busy taking in laundry, buckling at the knees, putting their faith in Jesus, mute and silent in their storm, to make history or even to appreciate the calling of Maggie the Ram, or the Aries that came after. . . . They called her crazy. (P. 153)

This representation of the bond between Hazel and her grandmother, and the similar bonds I have cited earlier, carries traces of the writings of Afro-American women from Zora Neale Hurston to Alice Walker and Toni Morrison. Moreover, the textual construction of such bonds is grounded in a pretextual ideology that views mothers, as well as mother surrogates, as sources of wisdom for young Black girls. Commenting on this practice, Gloria Joseph writes:

> Black women play integral roles in the family, and frequently it is immaterial whether they are biological mothers, sisters, or members of the extended family. From the standpoint of many Black daughters

it could be: my sister, my mother, my aunt, my mother, my grand-mother, my mother. They are all daughters, and they frequently "mother" their sisters, nieces, nephews, or cousins, as well as their own children.[14]

In its focus on male–female relationships, Gorilla addresses the issue of rejection, which is the inevitable fate of the in-dependent woman. In "Maggie of the Green Bottles," this issue is stressed in the "eulogy" delivered by Reverend Olson at Maggie's funeral. He points to her violations of the unwritten but implicitly understood rules of the community governing women's behavior, of her challenging arbitrarily constituted male authority and her overall rebelliousness. He suggests to a receptive congregation that she "must have been crazy." The "eulogy" becomes a medium through which the community's ideology, which defined and prescribed desirable female be-havior, is reinforced and a warning is directed to those women who might be tempted to emulate Maggie's transgression.

In "The Johnson Girls," the small community of women discovers that their strengths make them undesirable to the men in their lives, that their refusal to accept passive roles alienates men. Self-assertion "on the block" is viewed as solely within the province of males. Sugar, one of the women, re-flects:

A man, no matter how messy he is, I mean even if he some straight up basket case, can always get some good woman. . . . But a woman, if her shit ain't together, she can forget it unless she very lucky and got a Great Ma Drew working roots. If she halfway together and very cold blooded, then maybe she can snatch some sucker and bump his head. But if she got her Johnson together, is fine in her do, super-bad in her work, and terrible, terrible extra plus with her woman thing, well she'll just bop along the waves forever with nobody to catch her up, cause her thing is so tough, and it's so crystal clear she ain't going for bullshit, that can't no man pump up his boyish heart good enough to come deal with her one on one. (P. 172)

"My Man Bovanne," one of the stories in which a defi-ant, rebellious older Black woman is represented, is told from the point of view of an older woman named Hazel (thereby linking her with the rebellious younger Hazel). It focuses on a seemingly banal situation in which the woman is berated by her children for her "backwards" behavior, which includes dancing suggestively with a blind man at a political fundraiser.

Hazel's refusal to allow her critics to dictate her behavior clearly places her rebellion among those of other autonomous women and girls in the narratives. More important, through her commentaries on the social and political practices of "the block," she embodies a challenge to the dominant theme of the text, Black cultural nationalism, and thus creates a rupture in the narrative.

Pointing to behaviors she considers inconsistent and ex-ploitative, Hazel communicates her uneasiness with cultural nationalism and her perception of its weaknesses. Disillu-sioned, she explains why she feels that she and other working-class Blacks have been invited to the fundraiser:

Grass roots you see. Me and Sister Taylor and the woman who does heads at Mamies and the man from the barber shop, we all there on account of we grass roots. And I ain't never been souther than Brooklyn Battery and no more country than the window box on my fire escape. And just yesterday my kids tellin me to take them coun-trified rags off my head and be cool. And now, we ain't got black enough to suit them. (P. 4)

Such ridiculing and questioning of nationalist ideology and cultural practices permeate the story. Reprimanded for danc-ing too seductively with Bovanne, Hazel explains that she "was just talkin' on the drums," for her children "can get ready for drums with all this heritage business" (p. 5). In a scene in which she reflects on the pain she feels when her "politically correct" daughter seems to have lost all capacity for warmth and affection, Hazel observes:

"Oh, Mamma," Elo say, puttin a hand on my shoulder like she hasn't done since she left home and the hand landin light and not sure it supposed to be there. Which hurt me to my heart . . . I carried that child strapped to my chest till she was nearly two. We was close is what I'm trying to tell you. . . . And how did things get to this, that she can't put a sure hand on me and say Mamma we love you and care about you and you entitled to enjoy yourself cause you a good woman? (Pp. 7–8)

This critique of practices associated with cultural national-ism differentiates the story from others in its genre, particu-larly those written by Black males. The narrative's dominant themes—the rejection of stereotypical roles for women and elderly people, an emphasis on the need to balance political commitment with intimacy and warmth, and the highlight-ing of contradictions in the nationalist movement—mark the emergence of a dissonant voice in Bambara's oeuvre, a voice somewhat analogous to Helen Cixous's view of the emergence of a feminist structure of feeling as "the precursory movement of a transformation of social and cultural structures." [15]

If Black women in the collection are largely represented as having an emerging consciousness of their situation, as well as wanting autonomy and participating in rebellion, Black male figures are characterized by subordination, vulnerability, and demystification. Generally absent from the text are the famil-iar Black male cultural heroes of the period in which *Gorilla* was produced. Whereas Black male writers of the time gener-ally romantized rebellious ghetto youth, "militants," and Black spokesmen in general, Bambara, referring to them only in passing, creates a startling contrast. Along with the primacy of women's desires in the narratives, she reinforces the feminine and proto-feminist dimensions of the work.

Generally, when men and boys do appear in the narra-tives, they are dependent on women and girls. Hazel's brother, Raymond, who is handicapped, depends on Hazel for sup-port; Manny in "The Hammer Man" is emotionally disturbed; the helpless and blind Bovanne is nurtured by Miss Hazel; in "Talking About Sonny," the protagonist kills his wife because "something came over me." There are few exceptions to these representations of male weakness and imperfection. In only two stories are male figures predominant, and even in those, the men's stories are mediated by women narrators. "Mississippi Ham Rider" evokes a seemingly romanticized portrait of an archetypal Black blues singer, and "Playing with Punjab" sketches a streetwise Black ghetto male. The representations of both men have apparently legendary or mythical dimensions, but they are deconstructed and undermined by dissonant moments in the narratives.

In "Ham Rider," for example, the young Black woman who accompanies her white companion to the rural South to attempt to persuade the old blues singer Ham Rider to come to New York for a recording session is impressed by the blues singer's "jackboots, the original War-One bespoke overcoat, razor scar, gravel voice, and personality to match" (p. 50). These items are signs of Ham Rider's "authenticity." Nevertheless, this mystification of an "authentic artifact" of Black culture is cut down in the text when the narrator reflects on Rider's probable plight in New York:

And what was the solitary old blues singer going to do after he had run the coffee-house circuit and scared the living shit out of the college kids? It was grotesque no matter how you cut it. . . . Ole Ham Rider besieged by well-dressed coffee drinkers wanting his opinion on Miles Davis and Malcolm X was worth a few feet of film. And the quaint introduction by some bearded fool in tight across-the-groin pants would justify more footage. No amount of drunken thinking could convince me that Mr. Lyons could groom this character for popular hootnanies. On the other hand, if the militant civil liberties unions got hold of him, Mr. Charlie was a dead man. (P. 54)

The narrator totally dismantles the romanticized and mystified representation of Ham Rider that she has constructed. He becomes, not a larger-than-life embodiment of Black malehood, but a quixotic figure, manipulated and exploited by those around him. Her ambiguous reference to the blues singer's having about him "a legendary air and simply not being of these times" strongly reinforces that demystification.

A similar demystification of a mythical Black male figure

occurs in the story "Playing with Punjab." Punjab, whose very name is a sign of ferocity, represents a commonplace character in the literature and film of the 1960s and 1970s. Flamboyant, streetwise, and tough, he is a metaphor for the rebellious Black youth of the urban ghettoes. On the margins of the dominant culture, as well as the Black middle class, he is seen as a hero "on the block." The inhabitants view him with reverential awe. Hazel's description of him evokes that attitude:

First of all, you don't play with Punjab. The man ain't got no sense of humor. On top of that, he's six-feet something and solid hard. And not only that, he has an incredible memory and keeps unbelievably straight books. And he figure, I guess, that there ain't no sense of you dying from malnutrition when you can die so beautifully from a million and one other things and make the *Daily News* centerfold besides. (P. 69)

Punjab's vulnerability surfaces when he becomes infatuated with Miss Ruby, a white social worker the city has assigned to direct a community center on the block. Punjab's involvement with her interferes with his ability to see that her actions are not in the community's best interests. When she manipulates a local election so that the least effective residents of the community will hold positions of responsibility, Punjab destroys the community center, forcing its closure. Like other serious issues in *Gorilla*, the incident is narrated casually, but the mystification of Punjab, earlier supported by the narrator's stance, is significantly undermined.

What occurs in *Gorilla* is a subversion of the paradigms of representation that generally characterize the fiction produced by Black males committed to the discourse and ideology of cultural nationalism. Their works usually construct a Black male figure who embodies self-sufficiency and heroism; in Bambara's stories, these traits are subjected to a radical deconstruction. The male figure is demythologized and ultimately displaced by an alternative mythical construct: a questioning and assertive Black female, who signifies an emergent feminine–feminist consciousness.

Beneath the surface realism that marks *Gorilla, My Love* as a race-specific celebration of Black life "on the block," then, is a submerged text informed by an awakening feminine and proto-feminist consciousness. Bambara appropriates the signs of Black nationalist discourse and employs them as strategies by which women are empowered. Consequently, the apparent centeredness of the stories is dismantled, the nationalist and feminist themes standing in a relationship of tension and attempting to achieve conciliation.

The Seabirds Are Still Alive

Published five years after *Gorilla*, *The Seabirds Are Still Alive* significantly departs in both form and theme from the earlier work, but the tensions, ambivalences, and irresolution endemic to the attempt to synthesize Black nationalist and feminist ideologies are even more dramatically represented. In its insistence on addressing cultural nationalist issues, *Seabirds* carries all the traces of a nostalgic text, evoking a past removed by nearly a decade from its historical moment. Its intersection with a burgeoning feminist movement locates it within the matrix of one of the dominant political phenomena of the period. This juxtaposition of two antithetical ideologies produces narrative tensions between the nationalist enterprise and the surfacing of feminine–feminist desire and ambivalence. Even the dedication in the text—"This manuscript, assembled in the Year of the Woman and typed by Kenneth Morton Paseur and Lynn Brown, is dedicated to Karma and her many mommas: Nana Helen, Mama Swan, Mommy Jan, Mommy Leslie, Mommy Cheryl, and Nana Lara"—locates the work within the emergent body of feminist literature of the late 1970s and postulates an ideological framework through which its narratives can be examined.

Seabirds deals with increasingly complex political issues and reaches beyond the epistemological boundaries that circumscribe Black people "on the block" to encompass larger geographical, cultural, and political constructs. Its politics are largely inscribed in its representational strategies, which take four forms: (1) more complex constructions of women, stressing their roles as cultural rebels and political activists; (2) an enlarged and extended projection of the Black girl as a child–woman who embodies nascent cultural and political consciousness; (3) an increased marginalization of Black males with emphasis on their diminished importance; and (4) more intensified depictions of white males and females as disruptive forces in the community.

Women who are physically and spiritually a part of the political struggle are depicted as having made an uneasy commitment to the ideology of cultural nationalism, and they feel a conflict about having done so. For other women, political consciousness is still evolving. For both types of women, however, conflicts are not easily resolved. The feminist voice constantly interjects itself in these stories, challenging and sometimes displacing the nationalist discourse.

Among the women committed to the politics of nationalism are Virginia, the heroine of "The Organizer's Wife," Lacy in "Broken Field Running," and the narrator in "The Apprentice." Each is engaged in examining and evaluating the level of commitment demanded by the politics of Black nationalism. None abandons the liberation struggle. Nevertheless, all respond ambivalently to their roles within the social and political structure created by the totalizing enterprise of Black cultural nationalism. The text becomes the site of conflict and tension in which the needs and desires of the individual Black woman contend with those of the projected Black nation.

Virginia's fantasies, for example, are structured by her desire to free herself from the cooperative farm that has become a symbol of Black self-sufficiency, economic and political defiance, and racial pride. Her ambivalence is dramatically mediated by the narrator when one of the other women extends love and succor to Virginia during Graham's (Virginia's husband) imprisonment:

And now the choir woman had given her the money like that and spoken, trying to attach her all over again, root her, ground her in the place. Just when there was a chance to get free. Virginia clamped her jaw tight and tried to go blank. Tried to blot out all feelings and things—the form, the co-op sheds, the long gas pump, a shoe left in the road, the posters prompting victory over troubles. She never wanted these pictures called up on some future hot, dry day in some other place. She squinted her eyes even, 'less the pictures cling to her eyes, store in the brain, to roll out later and crush her future with the weight of this place and its troubles.[16]

Similar ambivalence is articulated by the narrator of "The Apprentice." Assigned to accompany a more experienced community organizer in preparation for assuming a leadership role, a young woman admires her older companion but becomes concerned about her own inadequacies and possibilities of perseverance. Reflecting on her role as a political activist assigned to work with Black teenagers, she wavers:

Being a revolutionary is something else again. I'm not sure I'm up to it, and that's the truth. I'm too little and too young and maybe too scarified if you want to know the truth. . . . It's just a matter of time, time and work. No sense in asking where though, you get a look. I could see it maybe if it was just around the corner. Then I could ask her to lighten up a bit. It's hard on me, this work. (Pp. 33–34)

Lacey, the narrator of "Broken Field Running," also perceives political activity as demanding; but her view is more cynical than self-doubting. Responding to Jason's metaphorical reading of political Black activists as the "last hunters of the age," the symbolic reincarnation of the "first farmer com[ing] down the pike and sett[ing] up a cabin," Lacey constructs a counterimage:

I don't know what Jason sees, but I see ole Cain in a leopard skin jumpsuit checking out the red neck and dirty fingernails of potato-digging overalled Abe; Cain, hellbent on extending the feral epoch just a wee bit longer, picking up a large rock and saying, "Hey, fella, come here a minute. Could I interest you in a deer steak, or are you one of them hippie, commie vegetarian homos?" (P. 51)

The cultural nationalist politics of the text dictates that these women move from questioning to accepting their roles in the political struggle. Self-realization is achieved only in terms of group racial identity. Significantly, each woman is represented as voluntarily attached to a community of lovers, friends, spouses, and children. Moreover, the demands for total commitment to nationalist ideology argue for the suppression of individual desire.

For these women, then, personal frustrations and their uneasiness with the demands of nationalism must be reconciled within the mythical Black community. Virginia commits herself to the task of maintaining the garden to feed the Blacks who form the collective. The narrator of "The Apprentice," after extensive soul-searching, develops the "correct" political position, accepting Naomi as a role model and committing herself to the struggle for Black liberation. At the conclusion of "Broken Field Running," Lacey embraces her community and its causes. These moments of reconciliation are presented as symbolic statements of intense personal and political growth. They represent a newly discovered "awareness" of political correctness—the total submission of self to the demands of the liberation struggle. But the initial inscriptions of discord and dissatisfaction in the subtexts of the narratives are not obliterated. They leave their traces as disruptive presences.

A second type of political Black woman functions metonymically, representing those in the community who are political exemplars. She is characterized as totally committed to political enterprises; indeed, she sees herself as a model for others to emulate. At the same time, she establishes links with the larger community. In "The Apprentice," Naomi is depicted as having the entire community under her care: young Blacks who are victims of police harassment, older Blacks alienated and isolated by age, and the Black masses in general. Hers is an engaged life; the struggle for Black empowerment, with its attendant political demands, is her raison d'être. The narrator graphically summarizes that engagement:

Naomi assumes everybody wakes up each morning plotting out exactly what to do to hasten the revolution. If you mention to her, for example, that you are working on a project or thinking about going somewhere or buying something, she'll listen enthusiastically, waiting for you to get to the point, certain it will soon be revealed if she is patient. Then you finish saying what you had to say and she shrugs—But how does that free the people? (P. 28)

Such total political commitment does not preclude feelings of warmth for others. For Naomi, this commitment is marked by selflessness, a complete surrender to the good of the community, and is stressed further in the narrator's mediations of Naomi's behavior: "[Naomi] views everything and everybody as potentially good, as possible hastener of the moment, as an usherer in of a new day. Examines everyone in terms of their input to make making revolution an irresistible certainty" (p. 33).

The same level of commitment, combined with tenderness and compassion, is represented by Aisha, the young Black woman in "A Tender Man." The story of Cliff and the political and personal dilemmas he faces are the primary focus of the tale, but Aisha, a "revolutionary" Black woman committed to the welfare of the community, dominates the narrative. Confronted with the reality of Cliff's former interracial marriage —a relationship unacceptable to any nationalist—and his failure to behave in a manner that she perceives as responsible to his daughter, Aisha calmly attempts to "correct" his conduct, even offering to rescue the daughter from the mother, a custody arrangement that Aisha finds wholly undesirable.

The relationship of personal and political commitment to the struggle is again presented in "The Long Night." The narrative is largely an extended interior monologue of a young Black heroine who survives being bludgeoned by the police because of her unwillingness to betray her fellow revolutionaries; her commitment remains focused on a utopian community of Black sisterhood and brotherhood:

They would look at each other as if for the first time and wonder, who is this one and that one. And she would join the circle gathered around the ancient stains in the street. And someone would whisper, and who are you? And who are you? And who are we? And they would tell each other in a language that had evolved, not by magic, in the caves. (P. 102)

These extreme examples of selflessness, the total submerging of one's personal identity and needs, are firmly grounded in the ideology of Black cultural nationalism. Enlarging on the patterns of self-denial that characterized the women of the first category, they speak to the political exigencies of the Black nation.

The Blues woman, while seemingly less directly engaged in the broad politics of the community, signifies rebellion on the personal level. Her primary action involves a movement away from the socially determined roles of a "lady" and toward full acceptance of her womanhood. She celebrates earthiness and eroticism, fashioning out of these a song that proclaims her rebellion. Her consciousness, as well as her social status, is distinctly working class, and her representation in the text assumes the form of a proto-feminist consciousness.

The most striking representative of the Blues woman is Sweat Pea, the beautician and manicurist in "Medley." A single parent, Sweat Pea works industriously to provide a home for her daughter. She has abandoned marriage as an institution, but she does not reject men. Eroticism is central to her mode of life. Although her economic independence is of paramount importance to her, she constantly celebrates the sensual pleasures of her life—bonding with other women, drinking, enjoying a jazz performance, or showering with her lover:

He'd soap me up and down with them great, fine hands, doing a deep bass walking in the back of his mouth. And I'd just have to sing, though I can't sing to save my life. But we'd have one hellafying musical time in the shower, lemme tell you. "Green Dolphin Street" never sounded like nuthin till Larry bopped out them changes and actually made me sound good. (P. 105)

Yet her submission to sensuality and eroticism does not blind her to the absurdity of male rituals, and she adamantly refuses to become entangled in them. When Larry, her lover, jealously attempts to curtail her freedom, she rebels, asserting that he is acting out "one of them obligatory male numbers, all symbolic no depth" (p. 115). She sees men's *machismo* in social arenas like bars as encounters between "gorillas," "man-to-man ritual[s] that ain't got nothing to do with me" (p. 116). And her refusal to be responsible for an alcoholic former lover by embracing the stereotypical role of a protective mother further proclaims her independence and heightened consciousness.

Honey, the vocalist in "Witchbird," is another representation of the Blues woman. Burdened by caring for her manager's discarded women and seemingly relegated to the role of an asexual matriarchal figure, she initially evokes sympathy and compassion. Yet in her insistence on controlling her stage life —from the content of the repertoire to the selection of her wardrobe—she emerges as a woman of considerable strength and independence. Moreover, her view of her art has a political dimension, for she sees in the blues a connection with legendary Black women:

I hear folks calling to me. Calling from the box. Mammy Pleasant, was it? Tubman, slave women, bundlers, voodoo queens, maroon guerrillas, combatant ladies in the Seminole nation, calls from the swamps, the tunnels, the classrooms, the studios, the factories, the roofs, from the doorways hushed or a dress too short, but it don't mean nuthin' heavy enough to have to explain. . . . But then the wagon comes and they all rounded up and caged in the Bitch-Whore-Mouth mannequin with the dead eyes and the mothball breath, never to be heard from again. I want to sing a Harriet song and play a Pleasant role and bring them all center stage. (P. 173)

Other constructions of the Blues woman can be seen in the women in the beauty parlor in "Medley," in Honey's entourage in "Witchbird," and in Fur Coat and Ethel in "Christmas Eve at Johnson's Drug N Goods." Behind their earthy laughter, sensuality, and rebellious social conduct lies a nascent feminist consciousness that runs as a subtext throughout the narrative, competing with the cultural nationalist ideology that informs it.

Although the young girls in *Gorilla* have come to a minimal consciousness of their status as females, their understanding of the political implications of that status is limited. *Seabirds* renders more complex representations of the lives of young girls. In these stories, the girls are specifically moving toward womanhood and developing a political consciousness that embraces both race and gender. This theme is developed in several of the stories, perhaps most dramatically in "A Girl's Story."

Rae Ann, the protagonist in "A Girl's Story," is confused and frightened by the onset of her menstrual cycle. Fearing the ridicule of her brother and the disapproval of her grandmother, she anticipates the event with horror. She equates menstruation with illness and death, associating it with foul smells and dark bloodstains. Her anxiety and discomfort are heightened by her grandmother's suspicions that Rae Ann has attempted an abortion. Rae Ann finds strength and acceptance through the invocation of the image of Dada Bibi, the teacher in the Black nationalist school she attends. Rae Ann attributes symbolic import to menstruation. While experiencing the physical changes she is undergoing, she reflects:

When Dada Bibi talked about Harriet Tubman and them she felt proud. She felt it in her neck and in her spine. When the brother who ran the program for the little kids talked about powerful white Americans robbing Africa and bombing Vietnam and doing ugly all over the world, causing hard times for Black folks and other colored folks, she was glad not to be an American. (P. 162)

In the context of these musings, Rae Ann's menstruation as a sign of specific biological change assumes the symbolic status of myth. As an indication of physical and emotional change, it points to her initiation into the world of women. And placed alongside her meditations on the struggle against racist and imperialist oppression, it marks the surfacing of nationalist consciousness. The biological change thereby becomes the medium through which the narrative represents the child's transcendence of innocence and initiation into a world in which the politics of race and gender occupies a dominant position.

Bambara's commitment to cultural nationalism would lead the reader to expect mythological representations of Black males in her narratives, but her fusion of feminist and nationalist ideologies in *Seabirds* results in the subordination of male figures. The drastic demythologizing that is central to the narratives in *Gorilla* is not present in the later collection; male figures are generally not in the foreground. Two men, Graham in "The Organizer's Wife" and Jason in "Broken Field Running," show strength of character and a commitment to the political well-being of the community, but they are contrasted with pimps, boy criminals, and emotionally detached and insensitive men. Only the older men—Old Man Boone, Edward Decker, and Pop Johnson—embody nostalgia for an idyllic past. In "Broken Field Running," Lacey reflects on their significance: "I'm really wondering where are the Pop Johnsons of my day. The elders who declare our community a sovereign place. Could raise an army and navy, draw up a peace treaty, levy taxes, declare wars, settle disputes" (p. 47).

"A Tender Man," the only story in the collection in which a Black male is the protagonist, reveals the ambivalence in the text. Cliff, although he apparently embraces Black nationalist rhetoric, dismisses his former marriage to Donna Hemphill, a white woman. He relegates her to the nebulous status of an "ex-wife" and refuses to accept responsibility for their child. His failure to confront his past actions and choices realistically is reflected in his relationship with the Black woman Aisha. Muddled by contradictory emotions when Aisha seeks to comfort and advise him, he has fantasies of physically abusing and sexually degrading her.

The title of the story is ironic, for what is represented in this "tender man" is a history, and perhaps a future, of destruction. Nevertheless, through Aisha's intervention and the inscription of a nationalist argument that every Black person is capable of political and spiritual transformation, the reader accepts the possibility of Cliff's metamorphosis. Yet the questions raised by Cliff's characterization haunt the text and challenge its central ideology.

Although *Seabird*'s focus on the gender politics of Black feminism results in a marginalization and subordination of Black male figures, its implication in nationalist politics informs its representations of white males. In several stories, white males are metonymic signs of empowerment that threaten the tranquility of Black communities. For example, in "The Organizer's Wife," although white characters are absent from the text, allusions to Black losses of property through the white man's duplicity and dishonesty, pressures placed on Blacks to sell their land, and incidents of arbitrary arrests and police brutality by whites suggest extratextual referents to racist oppression. In this textualization, related to what Eco calls "ideological overcoding," meaning is produced when the reader and narrator share a semiotic system and an ideological reference point.[17]

Tropes of metaphor and metonomy to represent a white male presence are used extensively in "The Apprentice," in which a policeman's beefy hand, a holster and a gun, and a carload of drunken white fraternity boys signify forces that disrupt the community. In "Broken Field Running," the destructive nature of whites is implied by the image of the Gothic cathedral that looms mockingly over the ghetto, the poor quality of housing in the community, and the prisonlike structure that serves as the public school. Similarly, in "The Long Night," clusters of images evoke violence and brutality: the sound of heavy boots, bodies being smashed, and a barrage of shots.

The sole white male who is given a name and a fixed identity in any of the stories is Hubert Tarrly, the pharmacist in "Christmas Eve at Johnson's Drugs N Goods." He is depicted sarcastically by the narrator:

The chemist's name is Hubert Tarrly. Nadeen tagged him Herbet Tareyton. But the name that stuck was Nazi Youth. Every time I look at him I hear Hitler barking out over the loudspeaker urging the youth to measure up and take over the world. And I can see those stark-eyed gray kids in short pants and suspenders doing jump-ups and scissor kicks and turning their mammas in to the Gestapo for listening to the radio. [Hubert] looks like he grew up like that, eating knockwurst, beating on Jews, rounding up gypsies, saying *Seig heil* and shit. (P. 201)

This "signifying," along with the metonymical and metaphorical representations of white males as embodiments of racist violence and oppression, allows the story to remain grounded in the politics of nationalism while addressing Black feminist ideology. Opposition to, and distrust of, the white world is clearly situated in Black nationalist discourse. Conversely, by subverting that strategy and calling attention to the personal narratives of the community, the story asserts its feminist voice.

The feminism advocated embraces exclusively women of color. The plight of the Black woman is in the foreground. White males appear only as reified forces of evil and disruption, and white women, except for an allusion to Donna Hemphill, Cliff's former wife in "A Tender Man," are absent from the narratives. The reader knows of Donna only as she is sweepingly dismissed as Cliff's ex-wife and an "unhinged white girl." Hence, while the introduction of Donna creates a possible context for exploring the problems of interracial sex and marriage, the nationalist ideology of the text forces silence and the dismissal of any such considerations.

From Storytelling, Folklore, and Jazz

The nationalist–feminist ideology in *Seabirds* is not solely generated by depictions of characters. It is reinforced by narrative texture and form. As a body of race- and gender-specific narratives, these stories draw on various Afro-American cultural practices—the oral storytelling tradition, the use of folklore, and the reinscription of Afro-American music forms. The incorporation of these practices is evident in the narrative structure, point of view, and semiotic texture of the stories.

Bambara has spoken and written extensively on the influence of Afro-American music on her work. What is most striking about her appropriation of jazz in *Seabirds*, however, is its role in emphasizing and reinforcing the ideology of the text. Jazz performances generally begin with a statement of theme, are followed by improvisations or extreme variations, and conclude with reiteration and resolution. An analogous pattern structures each of the stories in this collection. In "The Apprentice," for example, the narrative begins with the narrator's anxiety about her mission, moves to an encounter between a young Black man and a white policeman, then moves to a senior citizen's complex, and finally to a Black restaurant. It then refocuses on the narrator's concerns and reveals her resolution to remain committed to political engagement. In "Witchbird," each fleeting reflection of Honey's extended blues solo constitutes a comment on some aspect of her life —her career, her past relationships with men, and her overall perception of herself. And in "Christmas Eve at Johnson's Drugs N Goods," Candy begins by reflecting on Christmas and a possible visit from her father, moves on to individual episodes largely focused on characterizations of the store's customers, and concludes with accepting Obatale's invitation to a Kwanza celebration.

This mode of narration serves a significant ideological function. In its highlighting and summarizing, as well as its glossing over certain episodes, the text produces its ideological content largely through clusters of events. Hence, in "Broken Field Running," the renaming process by which Black children discard their "slave names" and appropriate African names to define themselves with the context of Black culture, the police harassment symbolized by the police car cruising in the Black community, and the destructive effect of ghetto life depicted in the criminal activities of Black males form a montage, a cluster of images each one of which might be said to encode a particular aspect of ideology.

The narrative perspective, particularly as it reveals the narrator's relationship to the text's ideology, also contributes to the ideological construct. In *Seabirds*, as in *Gorilla*, the dominant narrative strategy is the apparently unmediated response of characters to the world around them. A particularly striking example is Candy's response to Piper in "Christmas Eve at Johnson's Drugs N Goods." Speaking of Mrs. Johnson's monitoring the performance of her employee, Candy observes:

But we all know why she watches Piper, same reason we all do. Cause Piper is so fine you just can't help yourself. Tall and built up, blue-Black, and this splayed-out push broom mustache he's always raking in with three fingers. Got a big butt too that makes you wanna hug the customer that asks for the cartons Piper keeps behind him, two shelfs down. Mercy. (P. 198)

Another narrative strategy in *Seabirds* fuses the voices of the narrator and the character. The two are interwoven to produce a single voice so that the narrator identifies with the character. Here is the narrator's rendering of Virginia's mental state in "The Organizer's Wife":

And now she would have to tell him. 'Cause she had lost three times to the coin flipped on yesterday morning. Had lost to the ice pick pitched in the afternoon in the dare-I-don't-I boxes her toe had sketched in the yard. . . . Lost against doing what she'd struggled against doing in order to win one more day of girlhood before she jumped into her womanstride and stalked out on the world. (P. 10)

The first section illuminates the narrative's dependence on realism. As with Hazel in *Gorilla*, the first-person point of view allows the text to establish Candy's credibility and her authoritative position in the world she occupies. Her voice is "real," and it reinforces the text's declarative formation. The second section largely achieves the same end, but even more clearly identifies the narrator with the ideology of the text. This identification of the narrator with Virgina's condition as woman enhances and highlights the feminine–feminist dimension of the narrative.

Narrative structure and perspective are further complemented by the semiotic texture, or strategies of sign production, that inform the ideological context of the work. Since the major thrust of the collection is the awakening of cultural nationalist and feminist consciousness, clusters of signs keep the text grounded in those ideologies. The linguistic subcode itself, a reified construction of "Black English," becomes the sign of difference from the dominant culture and unity with the alternative Black community. In "Broken Field Running," Lacey, describing the wind blowing during a winter snowstorm, invokes metaphorical constructs and the syntax drawn from a Black cultural context:

The Hawk and his whole family doing their number on Hough Avenue, rattling the panes in the poolroom window, brushing up bald spots on the cat from the laundry poised, shaking powder from his paw, stunned. . . . Flicking my lashes I can see where I'm going for about a minute till the wind gusts up again, sweeping all up under folks' clothes doing a merciless sodomy. (P. 21)

Other strategies exist in a dialectical relationship with the text's primary enterprise, the production of Black nationalist and feminist ideology: the symbolic evocation of historical figures (e.g., Harriet Tubman, Fannie Lou Hammer, Malcolm X), the ritual of African renaming, and the visual signs associated with clothing styles such as gelees and dashikis. The jazz structure that informs the narrative and the blues motif used in

Honey's meditation in "Witchbird" can also be viewed as signs drawn from the culture of Black music and reinforced in the linguistic code.

A Synthesis of Ideologies

Gorilla and *Seabirds*, then, while produced at historically different moments, are both structured by the desire to synthesize contending ideologies of Black cultural nationalism and feminism. With its submerged text, its positioning of girls and women as primary narrators, its eruption of women-defined issues and strategies of marginalizing Black males, *Gorilla* disrupts the apparent unity of the world it seems to represent: an idyllic inner world of the Black community in which intraracial strife is minimal or nonexistent.

Seabirds identifies itself with the emergent feminist movement even in its dedication. The women in these stories possess a keen political awareness; the young girls have expanded their political consciousness; and Black male figures are even farther on the margins than they were in the earlier work. Tensions between nationalists and feminists are concretely presented in *Seabirds*, and the indeterminancy of the text is in the foreground.

The Salt Eaters, a work that bears all the traces of postmodern textual production, radically rewrites and displaces these earlier works. I discuss it in the final chapter of this book and show how its central representations of madness and disillusionment, the increased antagonism between the sexes, and the triumph of an alternative culture displace the ambivalence of the earlier works and project a vision that is both dystopian and utopian.

FIVE

◆

History and Genealogy in Walker's
The Third Life of Grange Copeland and *Meridian*

Aᴸɪᴄᴇ Wᴀʟᴋᴇʀ's ideological position stresses rebellion and liberation. Whether drawing on her involvement in the civil rights movement (an activity she views as "revolutionary"), or arguing that her fiction must speak to the "survival of the race," or advancing her program for a "womanist" ideology, her works address specific social and political issues. She succinctly stated her position in an interview reprinted in *In Search of Our Mothers' Gardens*:

I am preoccupied with the spiritual survival, the *whole* of my people. But beyond that, I am committed to exploring the oppressions, the insanities, the loyalties, and the triumphs of black women. . . . For me, black women are the most fascinating creations in the world.

Next to them, I place the old people—male and female—who persist in their beauty in spite of everything. How do they do this, knowing what they do? Having lived what they have lived? It is a mystery, and so it lures me into their lives.[1]

For Walker, a commitment to writing must be combined with social and political activism if it is to be of significance. Like Toni Cade Bambara, Walker views the role of the Black artist as multifaceted:

My major advice to young black artists would be that they shut themselves up somewhere away from all debates about who they are and

what color they are and just turn out paintings and poems and stories
and novels. Of course the kind of artist we are required to be cannot
do this. Our people are waiting. *But there must be an awareness of
what is Bull and what is Truth*, what is practical and what is designed
ultimately to paralyze our talents. For example, it is unfair to the
people we expect to reach to give them a beautiful poem if they are
unable to read it.

The real revolution is always concerned with the least glamorous stuff.
With raising a reading level from second grade to third. With sim-
plifying history and writing it down (or reciting it) for the old folks.
With helping illiterates fill out food-stamp forms. . . . The dull, frus-
trating work with our people is the work of the black revolutionary
artist. It means, most of all, staying close enough to them to be there
whenever they need you. (*Search*, 133–135)

In this chapter I focus on Walker's project of "simplify-
ing history," particularly the semiotic representation of history
in fictional discourse. Her first two novels, *The Third Life of
Grange Copeland* and *Meridian*, are structured by their inscription of two historical narratives: one focuses on the broad
racial experiences of American Blacks, without regard to gender issues; the other more specifically focuses on the histories of Black women. Walker's text constantly oscillates between these two discourses. The framing narrative, generally
grounded in racial history, is often disrupted and subverted
by the subordinate discourse that addresses the experiences of
Black women.

An argument can be advanced that would challenge the
reading of fiction as history, but modern scholarship has illustrated that such divisions are largely artificial. Hayden White,
for example, has convincingly argued that the textual strategies—modes of emplotment, tropological strategies, and the
like—are the same in the production of historiography and
the novel.[2] White clearly has shown the relationship between
history and fiction in his argument that "as verbal artifacts
histories and novels are indistinguishable from one another."

We cannot distinguish between them on formal grounds unless we
approach them with specific preconceptions about the kinds of truths

that each is supposed to deal in. But the aim of the writer of a novel must be the same as that of the writer of a history. Both wish to provide a verbal image of "reality." The novelist may present this reality indirectly, that is to say, by figurative techniques, rather than directly, which is to say, by registering a series of propositions which are supposed to correspond point by point to some extra-textual domain of occurrence or happening, as the historian claims to do. But the image of reality which the novelist thus constructs is meant to correspond in its general outline to some domain of human experience which is no less "real" than that referred to by the historian.[3]

White's description of the strategies employed by the novelist is directly relevant to Alice Walker's work. Generally covering four or more decades in her novels, Walker evokes specific historical events and personages, and her metaphorical and metonymical representations of the experiences of Blacks as oppressed people reflect historical consciousness. This focus on a general racial history locates her work within the tradition of Black male fiction. Yet that tradition cannot entirely accommodate Walker's narrative, for she is also concerned with the specific experiences of Black women, a focus that demands a feminist genealogy. Gayle Greene and Coppelia Kahn's description of the limitations of conventional historiography are relevant to the task Walker undertakes.

What has been designated historically significant has been deemed so according to a valuation of power and activity in the public world. History has been written primarily from the perspective of the authoritative male subject—the single triumphant consciousness—with a view to justifying the politically dominant west—individualism, progress, conquest—i.e., to providing pedigrees for individuals, rising classes, nations, cultures and ideologies. As long as the "transmission and experience of power" are its primary focus, as long as war and politics are seen as more significant to the history of humankind than child-rearing, women remain marginalized or invisible. Its androcentric framework . . . has excluded from its consideration not only women but the poor, the anonymous, and the illiterate.[4]

Inscriptions of the feminine in Walker's novels are marked by their difference from the racial history she invokes. Quite often, they become alternative narratives that disrupt or address, directly or indirectly, the omissions of the framing historical discourse. The peremptory movement of a feminine–feminist counterdiscourse becomes the dominant textual activity. These historical narratives of women, while contained within the framework of the racial historical narratives, become signifiers of sexual difference.

Greene and Kahn's critique of historiography is arguably focused on Eurocentric historical discourse, but Afro-American representations of history share characteristics of that discourse. The stress on outer-world/inner-world conflict, the emphasis on the public over the private and the political over the personal, and the elision of existential modalities within the inner world characterize the Afro-American novel in general as largely male centered. What one encounters in Walker's early works in particular is an inscription of that discourse, but one that is persistently challenged by a feminine counterdiscourse.

The challenge, then, for any examination of Walker's narratives is to explore the manner in which the two discourses are inscribed in the text, marking their points of intersection and divergence. Moreover, one needs to examine the manner in which the racial historical discourse becomes increasingly marginalized and is often displaced by alternative narratives of feminist desire. Central to these concerns is the role of the reader. How is the reader's subjectivity influenced by a text that oscillates between two contending discourses? How is the reader actively implicated in the construction of those discourses? To what extent can the reader infer a cohesive ideological project in Walker's fiction? I address these issues in my readings of *The Third Life of Grange Copeland* and *Meridian*.

The Third Life of Grange Copeland

Alice Walker has described *The Third Life of Grange Copeland* as "a novel that is chronological in structure, or one devoted, more or less, to rigorous realism."[5] That purpose is undercut by ruptures generated by the narration of competing histories. Although one might expect Grange to be the primary focus of the novel, he becomes largely a vehicle through which the broader racial experience is narrated[6] and is then displaced and challenged by previously subordinate narratives that focus specifically on the experiences of Black women.[7] In addition to inscribing the narratives of Grange and Brownfield, the novel commits itself to the stories of Mem, Margaret, Josie, and communities of anonymous women. The personal histories of Brownfield and Grange remain the dominant focus of the narrative, but the women's stories serve significant textual and ideological functions. I return to this issue in a detailed treatment of those narratives, but at the moment I wish to focus on the Grange–Brownfield narrative frame.

The ideological enterprise that the novel undertakes may be viewed as having two dimensions: Through her symbolic use of Grange and Brownfield, Walker advances the argument that the culture of poverty, with its racial underpinnings, is essentially dehumanizing. At the same time, she asserts that one has a responsibility to transcend that dehumanization. What is involved is not merely a symbolic representation of dehumanization but the constant intervention of an external narrator who comments and interprets for the reader, keeping Walker's argument in the foreground. The narrative, by shifting the centers of consciousness throughout the novel, aids her in this strategy.

Grange's "first life" is viewed by the child Brownfield, whose perceptions are refined and transmitted by the narrator. A congeries of details invites the reader to construct a picture of the sharecropper's life. The single image is integrated into a pattern that ultimately forms a delineation of the culture of poverty. Brownfield develops sores because of poor nutrition; Margaret is forced to work in a bait factory as her husband labors as a sharecropper; at age six, Brownfield begins working in the fields; the family lives in grossly substandard housing. A significant manner in which this Gestalt is constructed is having the sharecropping experience viewed through Brown-

field's eyes. The scene in which the narrator tells of Brownfield's reaction to Grange's fear of Mister Shipley, the white
foreman for whom he works, illustrates this:

Once the man touched [Brownfield] on the hand with the handle of
his cane . . . and said, "You're Grange Copeland's boy, ain't you?"
And Brownfield had answered, "Uh huh," chewing on his lip and
recoiling from the enormous pile of gray-black hair that lay matted
on the man's upper chest and throat. While he stared at the hair
one of the workers—not his father who was standing beside him
as if he didn't know he was there—said to him softly, "Say 'Yessir'
to Mr. Shipley," and Brownfield looked up before he said anything
and scanned his father's face. The mask was as tight and still as
if his father had coated himself with wax. And Brownfield smelled
for the first time an odor of sweat, fear, and something indefinite.
Something smothered and tense (which was of his father and of the
other workers . . .) that came from his father's body. His father
said nothing. Brownfield, trembling, said "Yessir," filled with terror
of this man who could, by his presence alone, turn his father into
something that might as well have been a pebble or post or a piece
of dirt, except for the sharp odor of something whose source was
forcibly contained in flesh.[8]

Brownfield's reaction to this incident, reinforced by the narrator's interpretation of it, places the episode in a broader
context, in what Hayden White has called the "domain of
human experience." The reader's response goes beyond the
particular experience of Grange to the larger issue of racial
oppression. Grange's response is filtered through Brownfield's
mind, and references to the other workers speak to its broader
implications.

This strategy of employing a single image to make a broad
ideological statement characterizes most of the novel. Grange's
total impotence is conveyed through physical description; the
reader must invoke a cultural code to interpret it. These descriptions may involve objects or persons, as can be seen by
the juxtaposition of a description of the Copeland house with
the physical description of Grange. The house has "rotting
gray wood shingles" and is marked by a pervasive grayness. It

resembles "a sway back animal turned out to pasture," and the surrounding area is marked by "a litter of tree trunks, slivers of carcass bones deposited by the dog and discarded braces and bits that had pained the jaws and teeth of a hard-driven mule." This bleak image is then reinforced in the description of Grange:

He was a tall, thin brooding man, slightly stooped from plowing, with skin the deep glossy brown of pecans. He was thirty-five but seemed much older. His face and eyes had a dispassionate vacancy and sadness, as if a great fire had been extinguished within him and was just recently missed. He seemed devoid of any emotion, while Brownfield watched him, except that of bewilderment. A bewilderment so complete he did not really appear to know what he saw, although his hand continued to gesture, more or less aimlessly, and his lips moved, shaping unintelligible words. (P. 13)

The two descriptions make up the broad picture of exploitation and dehumanization that the reader is invited to construct. The description of Grange illuminates that oppression, and it is made more poignant by having it filtered through the mind of the child. The reader can respond sympathetically to both of them and can experience rage at the conditions under which they live.

At the same time, an alternative narrative, centered on the oppression of the Black woman, is subtly introduced. Again, the reader experiences Margaret Copeland only through the eyes of Brownfield in a narration that is then mediated by the narrator. The reader is forced to construct a more complete narrative.

Margaret's oppressive situation is revealed early in the novel when she agrees with Grange during a family dispute. Brownfield's response is as follows: "His mother agreed with his father whenever possible. And though he was only ten Brownfield wondered about this. He thought his mother was like their dog in some ways. She didn't have a thing to say that did not in some way show her submission to his father" (p. 5). References to Grange's infidelity, his drunkenness and the terror it instills,

and his abandonment of his family follow. Because of his behavior, Margaret sinks into alcoholism and sexual promiscuity,
resulting in her having a child out of wedlock. Her death is
briefly described after Grange has abandoned the family:

"Well. He's gone," his mother said without anger at the end of the
third week. But the following week she and her poisoned baby went
out into the dark of the clearing and in the morning Brownfield
found them there. She was curled up in a lonely sort of way, away
from her child, as if she had spent the last moment on her knees.
(P. 21)

Margaret's story is largely contained within the dominant
narrative frame. Her suffering is represented as part of the
larger spiritual annihilation that is characteristic of the sharecropping system. The narrative strategy of having events filtered through the mind of Brownfield precludes a telling of
Margaret's story, yet her story remains a disturbing presence
embedded within the dominant narrative. Even at this early
stage, the text moves toward its own decentering.

In earlier chapters, the focus on Brownfield allows the
reader to sympathize with him. Brownfield the child is the one
we see as the primary victim of racism and economic exploitation. This procedure is followed as Brownfield assumes the role
that Grange had played before fleeing the South. The narrator invokes the same strategy of physical description to address
Brownfield's plight:

He had once been a handsome man, slender and tall with narrow
beautiful hands. From trying to see in kerosene lamplight his once
clear eyes were now red-veined and yellow with a permanent squint.
From running after white folks' cows, he never tended much to his
own, when he had any, and he'd developed severe athlete's foot that
caused him to limp when the weather was hot or wet. From working
in fields and with cows in all kinds of weather he developed a serious
bronchitis aggravated by rashes and allergies. (P. 83)

The physical description of Brownfield becomes the embodiment of the oppressive conditions under which the sharecrop-

pers lived. Disease, illness, and dehumanization underscore these destructive conditions. The details are presented directly by the extradiegetic narrator and invite the reader to respond.

The argument that such treatment does not justify abusing others is given even stronger weight in this section. Therefore, the movement away from Brownfield as victim to Brownfield as oppressor requires a shifting of the narrative focus. The reader must respond to the verbal and physical violence inflicted on Mem by Brownfield with a shift in judgment of Brownfield's character.

What was largely suggested in the Margaret–Grange marriage is presented in graphic detail in the description of the union between Brownfield and Mem. The larger history is subordinated as domestic violence dominates. Individual scenes record Brownfield's increasing brutality: Mem beaten and dehumanized; the children Daphne, Ornette, and Ruth living in constant fear of their father; the gradual physical and moral destruction of Mem. Brownfield's behavior forces the reader to withdraw from him. As attention shifts to Brownfield's victims, pathos becomes the dominant representation of the household. The Brownfield children construct an imaginary narrative about a more generous and kind Brownfield; and Mem, in a moment of rebellion, threatens to kill Brownfield unless his behavior changes. Whatever sympathies the reader might still have for Brownfield are eliminated in the narrator's description of Mem's murder (examined in more detail later in this chapter).

The focus on Mem as a victim of brutality and the responses of her children to that brutal treatment mark a move away from the original ideological purpose. As the text focuses more intensely on the domestic violence, the outer world recedes. The argument shifts its perspective—from Brownfield as victim to the women and children as the most victimized. At this point, the text reintroduces Grange, now older and wiser, as the antithesis of Brownfield.

The return of Grange, in his "second life," endows him

with larger-than-life dimensions. He is protective of his niece, Ruth, to whom he seems to be totally devoted; he is now the storyteller, the person who has traveled far and returned to share his wisdom. The reader is led to believe that Grange has undergone a major conversion. (Omitted is any detailed treatment of Grange's earlier desertion of his family and his cruelty to Brownfield as a child.) This change in character presents Grange as the embodiment of human possibility. At the core of Grange's transformation is the novel's ideological statement that one cannot be so dehumanized by a system as to lose one's own humanity. In a heated argument with Brownfield, Grange articulates that philosophy:

"By George, I know the danger of putting all the blame on somebody else for the mess you make out of your life. I fell into the trap myself! And I'm bound to believe that that's the way the white folks can corrupt you even when you done held up before. 'Cause when they got you thinking that they're to blame for *everything* they have you thinking they's some kind of gods! You can't do nothing wrong without them being behind it. You gits just as weak as water, no feeling of doing *nothing* yourself. Then you begins to think up evil and begins to destroy everybody around you, and you blames it on the crackers. *Shit!* Nobody's as powerful as we make them out to be. We got our own *souls* don't we? (P. 207)

This statement, while addressed to Brownfield, forces the reader to modify his or her initial response. The destruction of Margaret and Mem can no longer be attributed solely to racism; it is also directly related to the moral failures of the men. In this respect, the novel follows a conventional plot development. Grange moves from a state of disequilibrium, characterized by his abuse of those around him, to a state of equilibrium, marked by a significant change in behavior. Conversely, Brownfield becomes increasingly dehumanized. The novel does not offer any reasons for these changes in the men's personalities; it merely presents them. What is important is that these reconstructions of the characters of Grange and

Brownfield force a rereading and reinterpretation of the entire novel.

Near the end of the novel, Brownfield is placed in an even more odious light when he conspires with a racist judge to regain custody of his daughter Ruth. This pairing of the judge and Brownfield against Ruth and Grange further cements the case against Brownfield. The novel's violent ending, in which Grange kills Brownfield and then dies in a shootout with the police, heightens Grange's heroic stature, giving his death a certain nobility.

In the Grange and Brownfield episodes, then, readers participate in the production of meaning and the working out of an ideological position. The early stages of the novel are clearly focused on the dehumanizing aspects of racial and economic oppression. The novel then proceeds to focus on victims other than Black males. And the characterizations of Grange and Brownfield, two men marked by exaggerated qualities of good and evil, become signs of opposing ideological positions, with the narrator clearly on the side of Grange.

If the personal histories of Grange and Brownfield reflect some of the areas of conflict in Walker's ideology, the representation of Black women reveals even stronger ambivalences and ambiguities. Margaret's life, which is seen solely through the eyes of Brownfield as a child, leaves these ambiguities largely unresolved. Mem, although more directly represented, has her life viewed largely within the context of the abuse she suffers in her marriage to Brownfield. The most problematic representation is that of another female character, Josie. Here the narrator vacillates, at times sympathetic to Josie and at times not. For example, Josie's independence is both praised and derided in the text. All three women's narratives are part of the larger design of the novel, however, and their individuality is suppressed.

Margaret is largely delineated within the initial Grange–Brownfield narrative. Mem emerges not as a specific woman but as a repository of various traits and virtues. The narrator

stresses Mem's formal education, her physical attractiveness,
and her assertive approach to life. Although these things differentiate her from the other women in the novel and help
provide a background for her in which her goodness stands in
contrast to Brownfield's evil, Mem's personal history is not revealed. The reader experiences Mem solely through the intervention of the narrator; Mem's life, as depicted in the text, is
one of omissions and gaps. For example, amid all the verbal
and physical abuse that Mem suffers at the hands of Brownfield, *his* reaction is more fully delineated than hers. This can
be seen in the episode in which Brownfield ridicules Mem
because of her language:

> In company he embarrassed her. When she opened her mouth to
> speak he turned with a bow to their friends, who thankfully spoke a
> language a man could understand, and said "Hark, mah *lady* speaks,
> lets us dumb niggers listen," Mem would turn ashen with shame, and
> tried to keep her mouth closed thereafter. But silence was not what
> Brownfield was after, either. He wanted her to talk, but to talk like
> what she was, a hopeless nigger woman who got her ass beat every
> Saturday night. He wanted her to sound like a woman who deserved
> him. (P. 56)

The passage focuses on Brownfield. The simple image of Mem's
face "ashen with shame" and her acquiescence in trying "to
keep her mouth closed thereafter" are all that the reader knows
of Mem's response. The focus is even more intensely on Brownfield through a narrative strategy that Paul Hernadi calls "substitutionary narration." In this technique, Hernadi argues, the
point of view of the narrator is merged with that of the character so that the two become inseparable.[9] Hence, the description of "their friends, who thankfully spoke a language a
man could understand" and the observation that Brownfield
"wanted her to talk, but to talk like what she was, a hope-
less nigger woman who got her ass beat every Saturday night,"
although attributed to the narrator, represent the perception
and language of Brownfield, thereby placing the primary focus

of the episode on him. The intensity of Mem's rage must be supplied by the reader from the isolated images in the text.

This strategy is reintroduced when the text purports to represent Mem's despair. The reader gains a largely elliptical view of Mem's feelings as the text shifts immediately to Brownfield's response:

> She wanted to leave him, but there was no place to go. She had no one but Josie and Josie despised her. She wrote to her father, whom she had never seen, and he never bothered to answer the letter. From a plump woman she became skinny. To Brownfield she didn't look like a woman at all. Even her wonderful breasts dried up and shrank; her hair fell out and the only good thing he could say for her was that she kept herself clean. He berated her for her cleanliness, but, because it was a small thing, and because at times she did seem to have so little, he did not hit her for it. (P. 58)

The first three sentences sum up the isolation and despair that Mem feels, but the reader never knows the depth of her emotions. Speaking of Mem's isolation, this discourse rather hurriedly describes it, but provides no depth of feeling. Rather abruptly, beginning with the passage "From a plump woman she became skinny," the paragraph focuses on Brownfield's response.

This mode of narrative distancing from Mem's emotions is evident even in the scene in which Brownfield murders her. The entire episode is seen through the eyes of Brownfield and the children:

> She was carrying several packages, which she held in the crook of both arms, looking down at the ground to secure her footing. Ruth wanted to dash out of the chicken house to her, but she and Ornette sat frozen in their seats. They stared at her as she passed, hardly breathing as the light on the porch clicked on and the long shadow of Brownfield lurched out onto the porch waving his shotgun. Mem looked up at the porch and called a greeting. It was a cheerful greeting, although she sounded very tired, tired and out of breath. Brownfield began to curse and came and stood on the steps

until Mem got within the circle of the light. Then he aimed the gun with drunken accuracy right into her face and fired. (P. 122)

The paragraph that follows details the horror experienced by the children. Thus, except for an isolated comment on the "large frayed holes in the bottom of [Mem's] shoes," with the flat piece of paper protruding, there is no attempt to delineate Mem even at the moment of her death. She represents pathos in the text, functioning largely to highlight Brownfield's cruelty and dehumanization. Through reading about her situation, we are forced to reevaluate Brownfield and are seduced by Grange's argument on the need to maintain dignity even in a world of oppression. Such a textual strategy necessarily results in Mem's personal history remaining largely incomplete.

Josie's narrative is significantly more fleshed out than that of Mem or Margaret, but the ambivalence through which her character is constructed produces uncertainty in the reader's response. She is a composite of contradictions: Both independent and dependent, she exercises absolute freedom in the manner in which she conducts her life and at the same time is seen as eager to abandon that freedom; she is kind yet vindictive and petty; and she is both celebrated and despised.

A significant development in the narrative of Josie is the attempt to create a personal history. The narrator provides a context through which Josie can be understood, and the fragmentary pasts that characterized the narratives of Mem and Margaret make way for a more fully developed character in Josie. The physical and mental abuse she endures at the hands of her father and the men who exploit her sexually are graphically represented. The following scene presents a pregnant, drunken Josie lying on the ground, surrounded by her mother, her father, and men of the community:

Her mother stood outside the ringed pack of men, how many of them knowledgeable of her daughter's swollen body she did not know, crying. . . . Such were her cries that the men, as if caught standing naked, were embarrassed and they stooped, still in the ring of the pack, to lift up the frightened girl, whose whiskied mind had cleared and who now lay like an exhausted, overturned pregnant turtle underneath her father's foot. He pressed his foot into her shoulder and dared them to touch her. It seemed to them that Josie's stomach moved and they were afraid of their guilt suddenly falling on the floor before them wailing out their names. But it was only that she was heaving and vomiting and choking on her own puke. . . .

"Let'er be," growled her father. "I hear she can do *tricks* on her back like that." (Pp. 40–41)

This representation of Josie as a potentially rebellious woman suggests the archetypal Blues woman we saw in the fiction of Morrison and Bambara. As a prostitute and the infamous owner of the Dew Drop Inn, Josie is the embodiment of rebellion.

As it was she was born into a world peopled by her grandfather's male friends, all of whom frequented the little shack on Poontang Street where "fat Josie" (she grew large after the baby) did her job with a gusto that denied shame, and demanded her money with an authority that squelched all pity. And from these old men, father's friends, Josie obtained the wherewithal to dress herself well, and to eat well, and to own the Dew Drop Inn. When they became too old to "cut the mustard" anymore, she treated them with a jolly cruelty and sadistic kind of concern. She often did a strip tease in the center of their eagerly constructed semicircle, bumping and grinding, moaning to herself, charging them the last pennies of their meager old-age savings to watch her, but daring them to touch. (P. 41)

This passage marks a significant turning away from the dominant focus. A woman's individual history is related outside the context of the Grange–Brownfield discourse. Moreover, the themes of woman as both victim and victor and of woman as rebel are inserted into the narrative, marking the eruption of feminine desire.

This desire is depicted as Josie's triumph over her social situation. She is alternately lover to both Grange and Brownfield, and is totally in control of her life. But the text downplays that position through its ambiguous representation of her. The reader views Josie through the eyes of Grange and Ruth. After Ruth is adopted by Grange, the narrator provides us with this interaction between the family members:

At the beginning Ruth was jealous of Josie, for she thought maybe Grange found her pretty. But Grange also thought his wife was not very nice, and he said so, often and loudly. He said she lived like a cat, stayed away from home too much. Josie was one of those fat yellow women with freckles and light colored eyes, and most people would have said she was goodlooking, *handsome*, without even looking closely. But Ruth looked closely indeed, and what she saw was a fat yellow woman with sour breath, too much purple lipstick, and a voice that was wheedling and complaining: the voice of a spoiled littler fat girl who always wanted to pee after the car got moving. (P. 124)

Although the narrator's position is indeterminate here (the passage seems to approach free indirect discourse or substitution narration after the first three sentences), the narrator's mediation of Grange's and Ruth's responses to Josie clearly preclude a positive reading of her character. Grange and Ruth are the embodiments of virtue at this point in the narrative: Grange has been reconstructed as a sympathetic figure, and Ruth represents a mythologized future.

The undermining of Josie is directly related to establishing an oppositional relationship between Grange and Ruth and Brownfield and Josie. Grange, whose "one duty in the world was to prepare Ruth for a great and Herculean task, some magnificent and deadly struggle, some harsh and foreboding reality" (p. 198), and Ruth, the hope of the future, with her probing mind and overall intelligence are meaningful only in terms of their difference from others in the text. Their positive values show forth through the shortcomings of others. Hence, the reader is forced to see Josie, not as autonomous and rebellious, but as weak, mercurial, and petty. The identification of her with Brownfield stresses their apparent similarity.

In *The Third Life of Grange Copeland*, then, the larger historical picture becomes a containment strategy for the subnarratives that constitute it. The novel's dominant theme

—dehumanization and the "correct" responses to that dehumanization—totally structures the narrative and strategies of representation in the text. It is imperative to position the reader so that he or she will make the appropriate response to the history presented. Thus, the women become semiotic strategies, signs of suffering and oppression, rather than complex individuals with personal histories. With the characterizations of Margaret and Mem, pathos becomes the dominant trope, leaving limited space in which to comprehend their full personalities. With the representation of Josie, the text assumes a more radical pose, alternately presenting her as desirable and undesirable, depending on the exigencies of the text.

Meridian

Meridian, published in 1976, six years after *Grange*, signals a radical departure from the earlier work in its representations of history and its narrative strategies. Yet it is also largely a work in which an accurate reading depends on the active participation of the reader. Form becomes a signifier of a new consciousness. There are no chapters as such, and so the reader is confronted with mere descriptions of episodes: "The Last Return," "Have You Stolen Anything," "The Wild Child," "The New York Times." These episodes are generally not structured by any strict chronology, and it would be possible to alter the structure without affecting the meaning of the text. At least one episode, "The Recurring Dream," assumes a metafictional aspect:

She dreamed she was a character in a novel and that her existence presented an insoluble problem, one that would be solved only by her death at the end.

She dreamed she was a character in a novel and that her existence presented an insoluble problem, one that would be solved only by her death at the end.

She dreamed she was a character in a novel and her existence presented an insoluble problem, one that would be solved only by her death at the end.

Even when she gave up reading novels that encouraged such a
solution—and nearly all of them did—the dream did not cease.[10]

This literary consciousness abruptly moves the narrative
away from reality and draws attention to the textual process.
By repeating the "She dreamed" sequences, coherent representation ceases and narrative development stops; the reader
must construct meaning. Moreover, the text itself is ironic
because Meridian, the presumptive *she* of this discourse, *is* a
character in the novel. Thus the work as an act of writing and
a particular mode of discourse is highlighted.

This strategy is one of many that mark the narrative's attempt to disrupt coherence, to declare its polysemous character
and force the reader to construct meaning. Further indications
of this occur in the fusion of genres. For example, the mythological story of the Wild Child and the Sojourner tree is placed
within the framework of a narrative grounded in realism. This
total disregard for chronology renders the passage of time at
best a secondary concern. The shift in narrative focus, while
always mediated by an external narrator, is never in the strict
sense polyphonic. The passage from one episode to another,
one situation to another, forces the reader to reevaluate his or
her position constantly.

In its treatment of Afro-American history the novel is at
its most radical. Meridian is the medium through which that
history is largely revealed, and through her involvement in the
civil rights movement history remains a theme of the text. Yet
that history occupies a subordinate role in the narrative and is
often placed on the margins. For example, the violence of the
1960s, marked by political assassinations, is simply entitled:

MEDGAR EVERS/JOHN F. KENNEDY/MALCOLM X/MARTIN
LUTHER KING/CHE GUEVARA/PATRICE LUMUMBA/
GEORGE JACKSON/CYNTHIA WESLEY/ADDIE MAE
COLLINS/DENISE MCNAIR/CAROLE ROBERTSON/VIOLA
LIUZZO

(P. 33)

Following this recitation of names is a look at Meridian's specific response to the funeral of John Kennedy, and what is striking here is that, throughout the episode, the horror of Kennedy's death is experienced only through Meridian's reactions to it. The death also serves as the onset of the friendship between Ann-Marie and Meridian, which takes precedence over the larger event.

Presenting historical events in this manner constitutes a displacement of the larger public history by a privatized version of historical events. The strategy recalls Habermas's description of the relationship of modernity to historical discourse:

Historical memory is replaced by the historical affinity of the present with the extremes of history: a sense of time wherein decadence immediately recognizes itself in the barbaric, the wild, and the primitive. We observe the anarchistic intention of blowing up the continuum of history, and we can account for it in terms of the subversive force of this new aesthetic consciousness. Modernity revolts against the normalizing functions of tradition; modernity lives on the experience of rebelling against all that is normative. . . . This aesthetic consciousness continuously stages a dialectical play between secrecy and public scandal; it is addicted to the fascination of that horror which accompanies the act of profaning, and is yet always in flight from the trivial results of profanation.[11]

Meridian moves away from the ambiguous characterizations of women found in *Grange* and heralds the rise of the feminine. Racial history in general is marginalized here, noted only in the fact that Meridian is a civil rights worker. As such, it is secondary to the main body of narratives that constitutes the text. Meridian is the character in whom these separate narratives are held together, but their meaning and coherence depend on the reader's interaction with the text. Basically, they are articulations of a nascent feminist consciousness. Each narrative, although essentially self-contained, contributes to a Gestalt. Among the issues the narratives explore are the celebration of the female as other within the context of a new mythology; the deconstruction of traditional social and moral values, particularly those governing women's sexuality and motherhood; and the problems that are central to Black–white feminism. The reader must see each of these themes as a manifestation of an implicit feminist consciousness.

The mythological dimensions of the novel appear rather early, in the form of embedded narratives. These stories have a surreal quality and seem irrelevant to the text's main thread. Marilene O'Shay, for example, seems merely to evoke the real, but minor details that place her in a different light. In the following scene, her husband has her body on display in a circus wagon:

"Marilene O'Shay. One of the Twelve Human Wonders of the World: Dead for Twenty-five years, Preserved in Life-Like Condition." Below this, a smaller legend was scrawled in red paint on four large stars. "Obedient Daughter," read one, "Devoted Wife," said another. The third was "Adoring Mother" and the fourth was "Gone Wrong." Over the fourth a vertical line of progressively flickering light bulbs moved continually downward like a perpetually cascading tear. (P. 19)

The episode ends with the response of her cuckold husband:

The oddest thing about her dried-up body, according to Henry's flier, and the one that . . . bothered him most was that its exposure to salt had caused it to darken. And, though he had attempted to paint her original color from time to time, the paint always discolored. Viewers of her remains should be convinced of his wife's race, therefore, by the straightness and reddish color of her hair. (P. 20)

Marilene's narrative ends at this point, and the novel returns to an encounter between Meridian, Truman, and the children. Yet as the novel progresses, Marilene assumes a different significance. The banal descriptions of her as "devoted wife," "obedient daughter," and "adoring mother" become descriptions that imprison other women in Meridian's world, and the racial ambiguity signified by Marilene's skin coloring signifies the cross-cultural oppression of women. Thus, Marilene becomes a dialectical metaphor, subsuming the major arguments of the text.

A similar embedded narrative concerns the Wild Child, an abandoned child, impregnated and thus removed from the moral values governing the lives of the young women attending Saxon College. Her antisocial behavior marks her as the antithesis of society's norms. That she becomes a symbol of rebellion for the girls in the college underscores her significance in the text. The coupling of her with the Sojourner tree, the third metaphor used in this early section, reinforces the meaning.

A story about the power of narrative, the Sojourner tree recalls the storytelling of a mythologized Louvinie whose art proved fatal to one of her young wards and resulted in her having her tongue cut out. After the narrator relates the incident, the fragment of Louvinie's original text is repeated in its entirety. The narrative then focuses on the historical relationship of the girls of Saxon College to the Sojourner tree, and the mythological significance of the tree is enhanced.

These episodes are digressions from the larger struggles of the civil rights movement and deliberately place the personal histories of women in the foreground. The reader must establish the relationship of these apparently disparate narratives to an implied feminist discourse. The cluster of narratives all focus on problems of women's empowerment or, more accurately, disempowerment.[12]

These narratives signify the emergence of feminist themes in Walker's fiction. What we have here is myth as an alternative to history. This mythologizing, on the surface somewhat disruptive of the narration, becomes an integral part of the text. The reader must insert these myths into the text so that they are integrated into the total framework of the novel. The feminist discourse of *Meridian* unfolds through this insertion of myth and folklore in narratives that signify their difference from the framing text, with its emphasis on racial oppression and blind spots to Black women's oppressed condition.

The symbolic representations of disempowerment exemplified by the Marilene O'Shay, Wild Child, and Sojourner tree episodes invoke folklore; the deconstruction of motherhood, also central to feminist ideology, is pursued more directly. It involves the defamiliarization, or "making strange," [13] of the ordinary situations of women's oppression. What is undertaken is a demystification of the Black matriarchy myth, resonant with the critique of the ideology of motherhood that generally characterizes nonfictional and fictional feminist discourse. That myth is revealed through the fusion of Meridian's narrative with that of her mother. Another myth, of romantic love, is even more radically cast aside through the antierotic construction of Meridian's story. In both episodes, the narrator directly intervenes, strongly reinforcing the theme of the text.

The reader does not experience Mrs. Hill's anguish directly —her voice is generally not heard in the text; the narrator interprets the significance of her life. The narrator not only describes the problem-filled life of Mrs. Hill but, by appropriating her point of view, reinforces it. Representing Mrs. Hill as a woman "who had known the freedom of thinking out the possibilities of her life," the narrator points to the destructive nature of marriage and motherhood:

She could never forgive her community, her family, his family, the whole world, for not warning her against children. For a year she had seen some increase in her happiness: She enjoyed joining her body to her husband's in sex, and enjoyed having someone with whom to share the minute occurrences of her day. But in her first pregnancy she became distracted from who she was. As divided in her mind as her body was divided, between what part was herself and what part was not. Her frail independence gave way to the pressures of motherhood and she learned—much to her horror and amazement—that she was not even allowed to be resentful that she was "caught." That her personal life was over. There was no one she could cry out to and say "It's not fair!" And in understanding this, she understood a look she saw in the other women's eyes. The mysterious inner life that she imagined gave them a secret joy was simply a knowledge of the fact that they were dead, living just enough for their children. They, too, had found no one to whom to shout "It's not fair!" (Pp. 50–51)

Mrs. Hill retreats into "abstraction," a tragic woman whose life is marked by despair and paralysis. In that description, the text makes a declaration to which the reader can become passively receptive: that motherhood is inherently oppressive. Not only is this reinforced by the narrator's comments (e.g., "Her frail independence gave way to the pressures of motherhood") but in the identification of the narrator with Mrs. Hill's perspective. The broader implications of Mrs. Hill's state, its relationship to the plight of "other women," places the event within the general discourse on feminism.

Having constructed Mrs. Hill as a victim of her acceptance of the role of Black matriarch, a position reinforced by Christianity and general social practice, the novel shifts its focus to Meridian's rejection of motherhood. Again the point of view is that of the narrator who explores the intensity of Meridian's response to her plight. The banal scene of a mother affectionately embracing her child is totally defamiliarized in this depiction of Meridian and her child:

She sat in the rocker Eddie had bought and stroked her son's back, her fingers eager to scratch him out of her life. She realized he was even more helpless than herself, and yet she would diaper him roughly, yanking his fat brown legs in the air, because he looked like his father and because everyone who came to visit assumed she loved him, and because he did not feel like anything to her but a ball and chain.

The thought of murdering her own child eventually frightened her. To suppress it she conceived, quite consciously, of methods of killing herself. She found it pleasantly distracting to imagine herself stiff and oblivious, her head stuck in an oven. Or coolly out of it, a hole through the roof of her mouth. It seemed to her that the peace of the dead was truly blessed, and each day she planned a new way of approaching it. (Pp. 69–70)

This joining of the motherhood myth with fantasies of murder and suicide heighten the argument against a romantic treatment of that institution and compel the reader to view it from a different angle. Thus, when Meridian decides to abandon her child in order to attend college, her mother's view of her as a "monster" for doing so is not sympathetically received by the reader. Inscribed in the text, then, is a historical examination of Black women's changing views on motherhood: Mrs. Hill embodies the traditional position, largely self-effacing and destructive; and Meridian represents the emergence of a feminist dialectic.

The third body of narratives through which the novel develops its views on feminism focuses on the relationship between Lynne and Meridian. Their relationship as women who nurture and support each other is the basis of the chapter "Two Women." In this scene, Lynne's mulatta daughter has been brutally raped and killed, and she has turned to Meridian for comfort while waiting for her husband, Truman, who is Meridian's former lover:

As they sat they watched a television program. One of those Southern epics about the relationship of the Southern white man to madness, and the closeness of the Southern black man to the land. *It did not delve into women's problems, black or white.* They sat companionable and still in their bathrobes, watching the green fields of the South and the indestructible (their word) faces of black people much more than they watched the madness. For them, the madness was like a puzzle they had temporarily solved (Meridian would sometimes, in the afternoons, read poems to Lynne by Margaret Walker, and Lynne, in return, would attempt to cornrow Meridian's short patchy hair), they hungered after more intricate and enduring patterns. Sometimes they talked, intimately, like sisters, and when they did not they allowed the television to fill the silences. (P. 173; italics added)

The idyllic relationship of these women, with its suggestion of the emergence of a feminist consciousness, is rendered problematic by Lynne's shifting characterization in the novel. Her whiteness becomes a signifier of her difference from Meridian and the Black community in which she has immersed herself; and she is variously presented as naive, coarse, and victimized. In one of two chapters entitled simply "Lynne," her view of Blacks approaches a romantic stereotype:

To Lynne, the black people of the South were Art. This she begged forgiveness for and tried to hide, but it was no use . . . to her, nestled

in a big chair made of white oak strips, under a quilt called The
Turkey Walk, from Attapulsa, Georgia, in a little wooden Mississippi
sharecropper bungalow that had never known paint, the South—
and the black people living there—was Art. The songs, the dances,
the food, the speech. Oh! She was such a romantic, so in love with
the air she breathed, the honeysuckle that grew just beyond the
door. (P. 130)

This portrait of Lynne, coupled with her occasional expressions of disdain for Blacks in general and Black women
in particular, creates an ambiguity in the characterization and
makes the reader's response to her somewhat of a problem.
The ambiguity is heightened when the narrator identifies with
Truman's assessment of Lynne's guilt as a white person:

By being white Lynne was guilty of whiteness. He could not reduce
the logic any further in that direction. Then the question was is it
possible to be guilty of a color? Of course for years black people were
"guilty" of being black. Slavery was punishment for their "crime."
But even if he abandoned his search for Lynne's guilt, because it
ended logically enough in racism, he was forced to search through
other levels for it. For bad or worse, and regardless of what this said
about himself as a person, he could not—after [Tommy's] words—
keep from thinking Lynne was, in fact, guilty. (P. 149)

Had these reflections been rephrased so as to identify them
with Truman, the narrator would have been distanced from
them. But the fusion of Truman's perception and the narrator's reporting makes this impossible and, combined with other
negative portraits of Lynne in the novel, clouds her characterization.

A significant episode occurs when Lynne is raped by
Tommy Odds. While the rape scene primarily depicts the relationship between Lynne and Tommy—particularly Tommy's
role as rapist and villain—it also evokes complex social issues.
It alludes to the historical moment in which the Black consciousness movement displaced the civil rights movement, resulting in the marginalization of whites in the struggle for
Black liberation. In exploring Tommy's behavior, it develops

the ambivalent feelings that some Black men at the time experienced toward white women.

He had wanted to make love to her. Because she was white, first
of all, which meant she would assume she was in control, and because he wanted—at first—to force her to have him in ways that
would disgust and thrill her. He thought of hanging her from a tree
by her long hair and letting her weight gradually pull the hair from
her scalp. He wondered if that would eventually happen to a person
hung up in that way. (P. 157)

In the context of Tommy's having had his arm shot off
by racists, the rape of Lynne assumes special proportions.
His attempt to invest the act of rape with a larger political significance reproduces some of the cruder positions assumed by nationalist extremists in the 1960s, and the image
of hanging evokes the entire history of lynching. In exploring
Tommy's motives, then, the novel juxtaposes two discourses:
one focused on Blacks, particularly Black males, as victims of
racist oppression; the other on women as victims of rape, one
of the most extreme acts of sexist terrorism.

The victimization of women, particularly the act of rape, is
an issue central to feminist discourse. If the novel's racial politics demands that it explore Tommy Odds's behavior within
the context of racial oppression, it is also committed to in-
vestigating Lynne's status as victim. That issue is somewhat
ambiguously presented through the graphic detail of the rape
coupled with Lynne's commitment to the "correct" political
attitude, even at the expense of her own welfare:

There was a moment when she knew that she could force him from
her. But it was a flash. She lay instead thinking of his feelings, his
hardships, of the way he was black and belonged to people who lived
without hope; she thought about the loss of his arm. She felt her own
guilt. And he entered her and she did not any longer resist but tried
instead to think of Tommy Odds as he was when he was her friend—
and near the end her arms stole around his neck, and before he left
she told him she forgave him and kissed his slick rounded stump that
was the color of baked liver. (P. 159)

The novel's depiction of the rape as an act to which Lynne's sole response is an abstraction from self, from her own degradation and humiliation to an "understanding" of the feelings of her rapist, destroys whatever feminist argument the text attempted to advance. Coupled with her reluctance to report the incident to the police because of fears of the terror that would be inflicted on Black males in the community in general and her acquiescence to the sexual demands of all the Black males around her, the response makes her significance of woman as victim problematic. This depiction of Lynne is consistent with the ambivalent feelings that characterize Walker's other attempts to explore the possible union of white and Black women.[14] One becomes aware of the tension generated by a text committed to both racial and gender politics. As a white woman, Lynne becomes a signifier of difference and sameness. Her representational status within the racial discourse is compromised by her whiteness, while her status as woman places her in a common sisterhood.

Walker's two early novels, then, mark a point of intersection and a struggle between two discourses: racist and economic oppression and the victimization of Black women. In *The Third Life of Grange Copeland*, the women's stories are contained within a narrative of the strategies of survival necessary in a social milieu of racial and economic oppression; as such, the reader experiences them as largely elliptical and fragmented. *Meridian*, on the other hand, disrupts narrative form and displaces that larger history to focus more intensely on women's issues. The full articulation of a distinct feminist position unfolds in *The Color Purple*, which I treat in the next chapter.

SIX

◆

Rewriting and Revising in the 1980s:
Tar Baby, *The Color Purple*,
and *The Salt Eaters*

I F THE EARLY WORKS of Morrison, Bambara, and Walker are marked by irresolution, ambiguity, and ambivalence, the narratives produced by these writers in the 1980s, particularly their novels, signal more radical inscriptions of race and gender issues. Each novel is, in some essential manner, a rewriting of earlier fiction. While the problems generated by the conflicting issues of race and gender still structure each text, the modes of representation and textual strategies differ significantly from the earlier works. Moreover, the reader's role becomes increasingly complex as he or she becomes more directly involved in the production of meaning and ideology.

The processes that structure each of these novels are somewhat suggestive of Umberto Eco's concept of the "open work." Open works, according to Eco, always involve a dialectical relationship between reader and text in the production of meaning. Drawing from examples of modern music, literature, and drama, he concludes that

(i) "open" works, insofar as they are *in movement,* are characterized by the invitation to *make the work* together with the author and (ii) on a wider level (as a sub*genus* in the *species* "work in movement") there exist works, which though organically completed, are "open" to a continuous generation of internal relations which the addressee must uncover and select in his act of perceiving the totality of in-

coming stimuli. (iii) *Every* work of art, even though it is produced
by following an explicit poetics of necessity, is effectively open to a
virtually unlimited range of possible readings, each of which causes
the work to acquire a new vitality in terms of one particular taste, or
perspective, or personal *performance*.[1]

In *Tar Baby*, *The Color Purple*, and *The Salt Eaters*, the
reader's involvement in "making the work together with the
author" and exploring the "unlimited range of possible readings" become extremely complex because of the representational strategies and narrative techniques that the writers employ. In addition to illuminating the semiotic textures that
inform each narrative and reading the novels as rewritings of
previous discourse, the reader encounters some of the traits
or signs that Fredric Jameson identifies with postmodern discourse. Among these are pastiche and collage as structuring
devices; the emergence of a schizophrenic textual structure; a
displacement of history by "historicism," in which the past is
reread and reconstructed in the present; and a valorizing and
privileging of nostalgia.[2]

Perhaps one should avoid too readily labeling these novels
as "postmodern," but there must be a recognition that the
textual strategies that inform them find their resonances in
postmodern discursive practices. The break with previous narrative modes, particularly the emphasis on classic realism that
characterized some of the earlier works, and the deployment
of idiosyncratic experimentations with form signify new directions in each writer's works. While Jean-Francois Lyotard's
theory of postmodernism differs somewhat from that of Jameson, Lyotard's observations on the defining characteristics of
postmodern discourse provide a useful theoretical tool for in-
terpreting the most recent works of Bambara, Walker, and
Morrison. Exploring the relationship between modernism and
postmodernism, Lyotard observes:

The postmodern would be that which, in the modern, puts forward
the unpresentable in presentation itself; that which denies itself the

solace of good forms, the consensus of a taste which would make it possible to share collectively the nostalgia for the unattainable; that which searches for new presentations, not in order to enjoy them but in order to impart a stronger sense of the unpresentable. A postmodern artist or writer is in the position of a philosopher: the text he writes, the work he produces are not in principle governed by preestablished rules, and they cannot be judged according to a determining judgment, by applying familiar categories to the text, or the work. These rules and categories are what the work of art itself is looking for. The artist and the writer are working without rules in order to formulate the rules of *what will have been done*. Hence the fact that work and text have the characters of an *event*.[3]

Lyotard's description suggests the anarchic, but it can provide an effective starting point for the three novels I focus on in this chapter. The "event" of each text, that which had been previously "unpresentable" because of historic and generic constraints, surfaces in a manner characterized by a kind of narrative violence. That which is "imparted in a stronger sense" in *Tar Baby* is a more open dialogue on the politics of race and gender. In *The Color Purple*, it is the displacement of history and the empowerment of a traditionally disempowered woman. In *The Salt Eaters*, it is the radical deconstruction and the insertion of feminist discourse. Each text generates "searches for new presentations," structured by unique approaches to representation and narrative strategies.

Tar Baby

One possible reading of Toni Morrison's *Tar Baby* is to locate it within a general discourse, already present in the earlier novels, that focuses on the opposition between the authentic (Son) and the inauthentic (Jade). Such a reading would argue for continuity in Morrison's oeuvre, presenting her works as a unified, coherent whole. Yet *Tar Baby* signifies an ideological project that is substantially different from those of Morrison's earlier works.

The novel posits several binary oppositions and inscriptions of difference marked by dichotomies of inside and outside. Son represents an indigenous and mythical Black culture, while Jade becomes the embodiment of deracination; Margaret and Valerian, the sole white characters in the novel, signify racial difference; the Isle des Chevaliers, Eloe, and New York become geographical spaces in which character is motivated and desire is realized. These patterns of opposition, the emphasis on differences generally, structure the narrative and determine its focus. Of equal significance is the manner in which characters and their ideological positions are presented.

Margaret and Valerian merit brief consideration. Significantly, they are the first depictions of whites in a Morrison narrative, and one might be tempted to attribute a central role to them. A close examination of the narrative strategies Morrison employs reveals a strong suggestion of ambivalence. Morrison stresses their marginal status and their function as signs of racial difference through several modes of constructing and depicting them: their objectification of the Black laborers whom they employ; Valerian's almost stereotypical embodiment of the middle-class white male; and Margaret's insistence that "I am not one of those women in the *National Enquirer*," although she has a history of abusing her son. Their narrative is always marginal to Jadine and Son's story, and they become the white presence, the Alien Other, of the novel.

Margaret's and Valerian's characterizations are further undermined when the novel allows others to "read" them. One strategy employed is to allow a credible character to comment on them. For instance, Therese thinks of the couple while performing household chores for them:

It was true, she thought. She had forgotten the white Americans. How would they fit into the story? She could not imagine them. In her story she knew who the others were: the chocolate-eating man was a lover, the fast-ass a coquette who had turned him down; the other two were the traditional hostile family. She understood that, but now she had to get a grasp of the tall thin American who played in the greenhouse whom she had never seen clearly and certainly never spoken to. And also the wife with the sunset hair and milk-white skin. What would they feel? She realized then that all her life she thought they could feel nothing at all. Oh, well, yes, she knew they talked and laughed and died and had babies. But she had never attached any feeling to any of it. . . . What went on inside of them? Inside?[4]

Therese's thoughts enlarge her characterization and allow the reader to experience her in a direct fashion. More significantly, the use of free indirect discourse and the metafictional nature of the passage make the representations of Valerian and Margaret problematic and signify the underlying ambiguity in their characterizations. That Therese views events in the house as constituting a story induces the reader to establish a connection between that "story" and the larger narrative, the novel, in which it is contained. Moreover, her admitted ignorance of whites in general—"What would they feel?" "What went on inside of them?"—complements the one-dimensional manner in which Valerian and Margaret are presented. It is as if the novel is questioning this racial other within a larger narrative in which problems related to race are central.

Still another indication of the "othering" of Valerian and Margaret can be seen in Son's reaction to the row between Ondine and Margaret at Christmas dinner. Jadine, in her attempt to come to terms with the disturbance that has occurred, ponders the meaning of it, which leads to the following exchange:

"It means," he said, talking into her hair, "that white folks and black folks should not sit down and eat together."

"Oh, Son." Jadine looked up at him and smiled a tiny smile.

"It's true," he said. "They should work together sometimes, but they should not eat together or live together or sleep together. Do any of those personal things in life." (P. 181)

Son's observations remain unchallenged in the novel, and the issues he raises are not pursued after the exchange between him and Jadine. The status of his words as "truth" is reinforced by the credibility of his character, and not even Jadine, who might be expected to challenge his statement, seems to do so. This marginalization of Valerian and Margaret reinforces their peculiar status in the novel: Although they appear to be characters and are endowed with proper names and personal histories, they function primarily as signs of whiteness and difference.

It is within the dominant narrative, however, the Jadine–Son story, that the ideological text is most clearly revealed. One of the most significant strategies Morrison employs involves the rejection of a simple monologic articulation of ideology and the inscription of many points of view. This process is similar to what Bakhtin found dominant in Dostoevsky's fiction. The monologic discourse on racial authenticity in Morrison's earlier novels is absent, replaced by what Bakhtin describes in Dostoevsky as the polyphonic. He detects in Dostoevsky's fiction a mode of narration in which

plurality of independent and unmerged voices and consciousness, a genuine polyphony of fully valid voices is the chief characteristic of Dostoevsky's novels. What unfolds in his works is not a multitude of characters and fates in a single objective world, illuminated by a single authorial consciousness; rather a *plurality of consciousness, with equal rights and each with its own world,* combine but are not merged in the unity of the event.[5]

This dialogic–polyphonic structuring of *Tar Baby* is central to the presentations of Jadine and Son and the processing of an interrogative ideological position. Both Jadine and Son are shown from three perspectives: self-representation, descriptions and delineations by other characters in the novel, and mediations by an external narrator. While a surface reading of the novel would support the argument that Son's position and value system take precedence over those of Jadine, closer scrutiny leads to an alternative reading in which the positions remain largely unresolved.

In addition to Son, Jadine's "others," those from whom she is sharply differentiated, are the swamp hags, Gideon/Yardman and Mary/Therese, and the "vision of the woman in yellow." In their mysticism and implicit claim to Black onto-logical status, their authenticity is in direct contrast to her ap-parent deracination. That deracination, however, is narrated from Jadine's viewpoint. Identification with the myth of Black authenticity proves a problem for Jadine. Her cultural experi-ences and psychic makeup are essentially different from those of the "authentic" Blacks. What is in the foreground here is a woman who argues against (as she does with Margaret) the need for "blackening up or universalizing out." Very early in the novel, this problem surfaces when Jade reminisces about the lover she left behind in Europe:

I guess the person I want to marry is him, but I wonder if the person he wants to marry is me or a black girl? And if it isn't me he wants, but any black girl who looks like me, talks and acts like me, what will happen when he finds out that I hate ear hoops, that I don't have to straighten my hair, that Mingus puts me to sleep, that sometimes I want to get out of my skin and be only the person inside—not American—not black—just me? (P. 40)

The theme articulated in this unfolding of Jade's conscious-ness is central to any reading of her character. The reader who insists on placing Jade's behavior within the realm of some mystical racial politics runs the risk of missing a serious Black feminist issue: the need for Black women to construct their own identities without having to submit to a dominant myth of racial authenticity. This issue reappears in an episode in which Son accuses Jadine of "acting white." The source of Jadine's outrage is quite specifically focused:

"Oh God," she moaned. "Oh good God, I think you better throw me out of the window because as soon as you let me loose I am going to kill you. For that alone. Just for that. For pulling that black-woman-white-woman shit on me. Never mind the rest. What you said before, that was nasty and mean, but if you think you can get away with telling me what a black woman is or ought to be." (P. 104)

While it is possible that Jade's preference for Picasso over an Ituma mask or the "Ave Maria" over gospel music can be read as signs of inauthenticity, the novel does not suggest that her preferences are insincere. Instead, they allow Jade's character to unfold without the intrusion of the author or an external narrator. Indeed, it is quite possible that political issues grounded in racial and gender problems are suggested here. Jade's struggle seems to be against having herself "interpellated" by others. She resists the definitions of Black women constructed by others and proceeds in her own manner to construct an identity. Hence the discomfiture she is made to feel by the mystical woman in yellow and the attraction she feels toward Son are points in a long process of self-identification. Through Jade's unmediated voice, the reader witnesses a long, arduous process of self-construction.

The text employs similar strategies in its characterization of Son. Through the intervention of the external narrator, descriptions by other characters, and self-representation, Son surfaces in the novel as a Black male whose existence is informed by an ideal and authentic Black culture. Racial and cultural difference is his signifying trait, and the narrative reinforces that difference. The reader encounters what might be called an "excess of typicality" in the character of Son. His entry into the narrative is marked by a frightened Margaret, who can utter but one word: "Black." His social idiolect is largely monosyllabic and colloquial, in direct contrast to the largely stilted language of Margaret and Valerian, and his dread locks—later designated by the narrator as "living hair" —combine with his dark skin to structure his character as the semiotic embodiment of Blackness. That Son signifies race is accentuated in Ondine's description of him:

The man was black. If he'd been a white bum in Mrs. Street's closet, well, she would have felt different. . . . The man upstairs wasn't a

Negro—meaning one of them. He was a stranger. . . . And even if he didn't steal, he was nasty and ignorant and they would have to serve him anyway. (P. 87)

To Margaret, Son is the archetypal Black rapist. Her evocation of the crude image of "Black sperm . . . sticking in clots to her French jeans and down in the toe of her Anne Klein shoes" (p. 63) and her constant state of terror and anxiety generated by his being a "guest" in the house are connected with and reinforce the idea of the Black as a disruptive "primitive" other that is suggested by Ondine's reflections.

The narrator is distanced from the ideological position taken by Margaret and Ondine, but the women's credibility, particularly that of Margaret, is weakened by their representa- tions as signs of inauthenticity. In what might be considered a counterdiscourse to their views, the text offers other interpre- tations of Son's character. Viewed as perverse and subhuman by the women, Son is perceived as a mystical and mythical force by the external narrator and other characters.

As the symbolic embodiment of a quintessential Black male myth, Son's representation can be placed within a larger framework that includes similar representations in Morrison's earlier works (e.g., Ajax in *Sula* and Milkman and Guitar in *Song of Solomon*). From the opening of the novel, when Son swims away from the ship he has abandoned, to its conclusion, when he swims toward the mystical horsemen in the hills, the novel points up his mythic character. His community is a world of men whose lives speak to total existential freedom. In summarizing Son's life, the narrator observes:

In those eight homeless years he had joined that great underclass of undocumented men. And although there were more of his kind in the world than students or soldiers, unlike students or soldiers they were not counted. They were an international legion of day laborers and musclemen, gamblers, sidewalk merchants, migrants, unlicensed crewmen on ship with volatile cargo, part-time mercenaries, full- time gigolos, or curbside musicians. What distinguished them from other men . . . was their refusal to equate work with life and an inability to stay anywhere for long. Some were Huck Finns; some Nigger Jims. Others were Calibans, Staggerlees and John Henrys. Anarchic, wandering, they read about their hometowns in the pages of out-of-town newspapers. (P. 142)

He is further romanticized and mythologized by the text's identification of him with all the signs that suggest the natural and mystical. The subculture occupied by Therese and Gideon becomes an extension of home for him; he shares camaraderie with the swamp women; he is identified with the woman in "the canary yellow dress," herself a mythological construct; and for him, Jadine's sealskin coat conjures up images of the death of "lambs, chickens, tuna, children, the slaughter of whole families in their sleep" (p. 112).

When Son tells his own story, he anchors himself in the discourse of Black mythology even more specifically. To Jadine's query about his future—"What do you want out of life?" —he replies by recalling a symbolic moment in his past personal history:

"My original dime," he said. "The one San Francisco gave me for cleaning a tub of sheephead." He was half sitting, half lying, propped upon his elbow facing her with the sky-blue sky of the sky behind him. "Nothing I ever earned since was like that dime," he said. "That was the best money in the world and the only real money I ever had. Even better than the seven hundred and fifty dollars I won one time at craps. Now that felt good, you know what I mean, but not like that original dime did." (P. 145)

This nostalgic evocation of the past, combined with other mythological constructions of Son, reinforce his status as the sign of racial authenticity. When Jadine questions the value of the culture of which Son is a product, he articulates a position that clearly demarcates the cultural differences between them and praises his status as a "real" Black:

The truth is that whatever you learned in those colleges that didn't include me ain't shit. What did they teach you about me? What tests did they give? Did they tell you what I was like, did they tell you

what was on my mind? Did they describe me to you? Did they tell
you what was in my heart? If they didn't teach you that, they didn't
teach you nothing about yourself. And you don't know anything,
anything at all about your children and anything at all about your
mamma and pappa. You find out about me, you educated nitwit!
(Pp. 227–228)

The contrasts between Jadine and Son constitute the dialogic dimension of the novel. Even their responses to places
reinforce their difference: Jadine views New York as "home
. . . a black woman's town" (p. 191); Son experiences it as
the site of cultural death, where "black girls [are] crying on
busses" and black men "had found the whole business of being
black and men at the same time too difficult and so they'd
dumped it" (p. 186). Their differences are further reinforced
when, after a night of intimacy with Son, Jadine imagines the
room haunted by all the presences of "Rosa and Therese and
Son's dead mother and Sally Sarah Sadie Brown and Ondine
and Soldier's wife Ellen and Francine from the mental institution and her own dead mother and even the woman in yellow"
(p. 222), all symbols of "authentic" Black women. Once she
rejects the claims of these women to a privileged ontological
status, she proceeds to reject Eloe as a meaningful social and
cultural construct. Jadine's perceptions of Eloe are mediated
by the narrator as if they represented an epiphany:

Eloe was rotten and more boring than ever. A burnt-out place. There
was no life there. Maybe a past but definitely no future and finally
there was no interest. All that Southern small-town romanticism was
a lie, a joke, kept secret by people who could not function elsewhere.
An excuse to fish. (P. 223)

This rejection of Eloe represents Jadine's rejection of everything implied by it: the myth of an authentic Black existential
modality, reified Black womanhood produced by that myth,
and Son as the romanticized Black male. The separation between her and Son at the conclusion of the novel is the direct
product of the irreconcilability of their respective value sys-

tems. Yet the reader should not too quickly conclude that the ideology of Black authenticity is necessarily valorized.

What has emerged from the novel is the inscription of differences within a dialogic context. While it is true that Son's character frames the narrative, both voices are given equal weight. The consciousness of Jadine and Son unfolds, privately and individually, sometimes mediated by an external narrator and sometimes through their own voices. The narrator's perspective is often suppressed, and the narrative opens itself to a plurality of meanings. Attempts to determine a single ideological position are futile because of the essential interrogative nature of the novel. Therefore, while a reading of *Tar Baby* that focuses on the racial myth would be possible to support, an alternative interpretation is also possible. One might argue that within a narrative that includes the politics of race, class, and gender, Toni Morrison brings to the fore an issue largely marginalized or even suppressed in her earlier works: the contentiousness between the desires of the mythical community and those of the Black woman whose existence is structured by historical and social circumstances different from those of the community. Jadine can be said to represent what had previously been "unpresentable," the individual Black woman who deconstructs the notion of "the Black Woman," a fictive construction generated by the ideological desires of a mythical community.

The Color Purple

If in *Tar Baby* Morrison modifies and elaborates on the feminist issues generated in her earlier works, Alice Walker in *The Color Purple* engages in a significant rewriting and rethinking of the issues presented in *Grange* and *Meridian*. It is not soley Celie's self-narration that designates the work as a specific feminist discourse but a combination of factors. The experimentation with form, particularly the appropriation and modification of the epistolary form, and the displacement of broad issues of Afro-American history by a specific feminist ideology largely characterized by images and representations that force the reader to reconsider the plight of the Black woman as oppressed, contribute to the novel's ranking as a significant cultural intervention.

The epigraphs ("To the Spirit: Without whose assistance/ Neither this book/Nor I/Would have been/Written" and "Show me how to do like you/Show me how to do it—Stevie Wonder") and what might be considered the envoi ("I thank everybody in this text for coming. A. W., author and medium") not only call attention to the novel's status as written work but, through the invocation to the Spirit/spirits, establish a relationship between the novel and some pretextual mystical discourse. This is strongly reinforced by the writer's representation of herself as one who "[has] been written" and as both author and medium. Moreover, the citation of Stevie Wonder locates the text in the realm of popular culture, particularly the unwritten body of folk practices that constitute the oral culture.

The most radical experiment is the novel's appropriation and reconstruction of the epistolary form. Celie's early "letters" are all written to what she later realizes is a nonexistent God; they are closely related to a process of self-narration and presentation through an extensive interior monologue. There is no dialogue between Celie and the Other—God remains silent—but a particular woman's history unfolds. The letters present a paradox: The apparent addressee, God, does not respond to them; the reader is almost a *voyeur* in relationship to them; and they become primarily self-narration rather than messages sent to someone.

The epistolary form is further complicated by the interjection of verbal discourse. The restrictive code in which the author has Celie narrate her story carries all the traces of the oral, although it purports to be written. Consider the opening letter, addressed to "Dear God":

My mamma dead. She die screaming and cussing. She scream at me. She cuss at me. I'm big. I can't move fast enough. By the time I get back from the well, the water be warm. By time I git the tray ready the food be cold. By time I git all the children ready for school it be dinner time. He don't say nothing. He set there holding her hand an crying, talking bout don't leave me, don't go.[6]

The rhythm of the sentences and the spelling strongly suggest dialogue rather than narration. Moreover, the entire novel assumes significance as social discourse grounded in problems of class and race. The reader decodes this language as a representation of Black folk speech. As such, it delineates Celie's racial and cultural status. The writing–speech signifies marginality and difference, allowing Celie to *describe* the oppressive conditions under which she lives and inviting the reader to analyze and interpret those descriptions.

The letters from Nettie to Celie continue the use of the epistolary form. Like Celie's letters, they too initially constitute a monologue, for while addressed to Celie, "Mister's" interception of them precludes any possibility of dialogue. What is striking is that when the letters move from addressing personal issues (e.g., both women's relationship to Mister) to representing Africa, they shift from a monologue to a somewhat self-conscious narration. Nettie's first letter is not substantively different from Celie's letters:

Dear Celie,
You've got to fight and get away from Albert. He ain't no good. When I left you all's house, walking, he followed me on his horse. When we was well out of sight of the house he caught up with me and started trying to talk. You know how he do. You sure is looking fine, Miss Nettie, and stuff like that. I tried to ignore him and walk faster, but my bundles was heavy and the sun was hot. After while I had to rest, and that's when he got down from his horse and started to try to kiss me, and drag me back in the woods. (P. 119)

Although slight differences can be seen between this letter and those written by Celie, Nettie's letter is still primarily oral rather than written discourse. The conversational tone, the disregard for grammar, and the incorporation of colloquialisms link it to the ordinary speech of the culture and class to which both Nettie and Celie belong. In contrast, an excerpt from a letter in which Nettie describes the building of the road in the Olinka village suggests a consciousness of writing technique and a change in Nettie's ability to describe and interpret her surroundings:

Every day now the villagers gather at the edge of the village near the cassava fields and watch the building of the road. And watching them, some on their stools and some squatted down on their haunches, all chewing cola nuts and making patterns in the dirt, I feel a great surge of love for them. For they do not approach the roadbuilders empty-handedly. . . . Each day since they saw the road's approach they have been stuffing the road builders with goat meat, millet mush, baked yam, and cassava, cola nuts and palm wine. Each day is like a picnic, and I believe many friendships have been made, although the roadbuilders are from a different tribe some distance to the North and nearer the coast, and their language is somewhat different. I don't understand it, anyway, though the people of Olinka seem to. But they are clever people about most things, and understand new things very quickly. (P. 151)

The complex sentence structure, the careful selection of ethnographic details, and the introduction of words that suggest intimacy, distance, and a sense of worldliness ("I feel a great surge of love for them," "their language is somewhat different," and "they are clever people about most things") distinguish this passage as written discourse and imply a transformation in Nettie's character.

In addition to their being experimentations with the epistolary form, these letters echo Bakhtin's concept of the chronotope, a term he uses to denote time–space relationships within narratives. Celie, who remains bound by the time and space of her community, does not alter her language even after coming to a heightened awareness of her situation. Nettie, who travels abroad and experiences adventure-time, requires a different language. Both characters, however, remain grounded in their private relationship. Bakhtin discusses this particular mode of discourse in his examination of the "contradiction [that] developed between the public nature of the literary form and the private nature of its content" that marked the Hellenistic era and resulted in the emergence of the "ancient novel":

> The literature of private life is essentially a literature of snooping about, of overhearing "how others live." This life may be exposed and made public in a criminal trial, either directly, by inserting the trial into the novel . . . , by inserting criminal activities into private life, or circumstantially and conditionally, in a half-hidden way, by utilizing eyewitness accounts, confessions of the accused, court documents, evidence, investigative hunches, and so forth. And finally we encounter those forms of self-revelation that occur in the ordinary course of our everyday lives: the personal letter, the intimate diary, the confession.[7]

Both Celie's and Nettie's letters reveal "forms of self-revelation that occur in the ordinary course of [their] everyday lives," yet they relate two very different bodies of experiences, which eventually intersect to produce a discourse on the plight of Black women. As I have suggested, Celie's letters are generally focused on self-narration and representation, while Nettie's are largely ethnographic readings of African culture. The two sets of letters together present the novel's ideology. The reader must establish the connection between these two groups of letters in order to grasp the ideology of the text.

Celie's letters are not only self-narration and representation; they are a textual strategy by which the larger Afro-American history, focused on racial conflict and struggle, can be marginalized by its absence from the narrative. Unlike *The Third Life of Grange Copeland*, in which that history is a containment strategy, or *Meridian*, in which it is a constant point of reference, *The Color Purple* primarily focuses on Celie's story. Her narration of her private life preempts the exploration of the public lives of Blacks. "First time I think about the world/What the world got to do with anything, I think" (p. 61). This reflection by Celie, at an early moment in the novel, is suggestive of the overall theme of the book. This restriction of focus to Celie's consciousness enables the novel to erase the public history and permits Celie to tell her own story.

This self-described "black, pore, and ugly" woman, with all the suggestions of race, class, and gender oppression implied in that description,[8] represents the suppressed voices of Margaret, Mem, and other anonymous women of Walker's earlier novels, and through strategies of representation and defamiliarization, highlights their status as oppressed.[9]

The presentation of the family as the site of oppression is a major defamiliarizing strategy of the novel. This is particularly evident in Celie's narration of the sexual episodes in her life. The graphic description of Celie's rape by her stepfather forces the reader to confront the ugliness of child abuse:

He never had a kine word to say to me. Just say You gonna do what your mammy wouldn't. First he put his thing up gainst my hip and sort of wiggle it around. Then he grab hold my titties. Then he push his thing inside my pussy. When that hurt, I cry. He start to choke me, saying You better shut up and git used to it. (P. 11)

Celie's narration of her moments of marital sexual involvement with Mister/Albert represents a similar dehumanization, one in which the conjugal act assumes the form of rape: "My mamma die. . . . My sister Nettie run away. Mr. ——— come git me to take care of his rotten children. He never ast me nothing bout myself. He clam on top of me and fuck and fuck, even when my head bandaged. Nobody ever love me, I say" (p. 109).

The two passages appropriate the signs of pornography and reinscribe them as signifiers of the antierotic. Rape, within or outside marriage, is totally demystified and seen as an instrument of oppression. The crudeness of the language and the graphic nature of the descriptions reinforce the dehumanizing aspects of the act. While Celie can narrate but can understand only in a limited manner the extent of her oppression, her narrative allows the text to construct, and the reader to decode, the feminist discourse underpinning the narration.[10]

Celie's narration of the oppressive nature of domestic

chores and her representations of male dominance and domestic violence further develop the underlying feminist, or
"womanist," discourse of the novel. In the inscription of lesbianism, however, the work most radically departs from Walker's
earlier novels. While it is arguable that *The Color Purple* is *primarily* and *exclusively* a celebration of lesbianism, in a broader
sense it can be encoded as a potential source of empowerment
for women.

The specific relationship of lesbianism to "womanist" ideology in general and, as a corollary, to its representation in *The
Color Purple* in particular is strongly implied in one of Walker's
essays. After surveying and celebrating recent literature produced by Black lesbians and discussing the hostility directed
toward that literature, she concludes: "*We are all lesbians*. For
surely it is better to be thought a lesbian, and to say and write
your life exactly as you experience it, than to be a token "pet"
black woman for those whose contempt for our autonomous
existence makes them a menace to human life" (*Search*, 289).

This elaboration of the term *lesbian* implies a powerful
ideological appropriation and redefinition of it. Rescued from
its devalued status as a sign of deficiency, it is invested with
broad political significance. The association of lesbianism with
"writ[ing] your life exactly as you experience it" instead of
being a " 'pet' black woman," and the further equation of lesbianism with living an "autonomous existence," transform it
into a sign of women's empowerment. This is the ideological
project that the relationship between Celie and Shug Avery in
The Color Purple represents and reproduces.

Any limited focus on the homoerotic aspect of the involvement between the two women runs the risk of downplaying
the complexity of Shug's representational status and its broad
symbolic implications. In her chosen career as a blues singer,
her refusal to settle for a life of domesticity, and her insistence
on enjoying all the sexual freedoms generally limited to men,
Shug becomes the embodiment of feminist existential freedom. More important, her character functions in the text not

only as the antithesis of Celie but as a vehicle through which Celie becomes conscious of, and empowered to address, the conditions that oppress her.

Lesbianism, then, becomes an essential aspect of "woman-ist" theory and praxis, encoded in the novel through Shug or, more specifically, through the bonding between Shug and Celie.[11] Whether invoking "Mister's" name, Albert, or leading Celie to reexamine her relationship to an anthropomorphic God, or providing her with Nettie's letters, which Mister/ Albert has hidden, Shug becomes an empowering agent for Celie. This is strongly suggested in the scene in which Shug, after arguing that "it pisses God off if you walk by the color purple in a field somewhere and don't notice it," presents a cos-mography to Celie that forces her to reevaluate her personal world view and come to terms with her oppression:

Man corrupt everything, say Shug. He on our box of grits, in your head, and all over the radio. He try to make you think he every-where. Soon as you think he everywhere, you think he God. But he ain't. Whenever you trying to pray, and man plop himself on the other end of it, tell him to git lost, say Shug. Conjure up flowers, wind, water, a big rock. (P. 79)

Shug's role, then, is one of effecting change in Celie's char-acter by bringing about a transformation that will allow her to extricate herself from her oppressive situation. The association of "purple," a polysemous sign,[12] with Shug, places her char-acter at the center of the novel's ideological enterprise: the processing of a "womanist" ideology. The erotic episode, with its tenderness and caring, contrasts with the brutality that per-vades the heterosexual unions and represents only one aspect of lesbianism in the novel; it also suggests a larger discourse of the possibility of women's autonomy.

Nettie's letters, with their ethnographic focus, demytholo-gize the construction of Africa as a utopia untroubled by any-thing other than imperialist exploitation. More directly related to my present focus, however, is the process in which those letters explore gender oppression on the African continent. This is graphically illustrated in Nettie's narration of an incident in which she questioned the Olinka about the status of girls in their village:

The Olinka do not believe girls should be educated. When I asked a mother why she thought this, she said: A girl is nothing to herself; only to her husband can she become something.
    What can she become? I asked.
    Why, she said, the mother of his children.
    But I am not the mother of anybody's children, I said, and I am something.
    You are not much, she said. (Pp. 144–145)

Nettie's letters form a counterdiscourse that undermines prevalent myths of Africa. This becomes even more evident as Nettie examines various African cultural practices, including clitoridectomy. Directly addressing the disempowered conditions [13] under which African women live, she observes:

Samuel [assumes] that since the women are friends and will do anything for one another . . . and since they gossip and nurse each other's children, they must be happy with things as they are. But many of the women rarely spend time with their husbands. Some of them were promised to old or middle-aged men at birth. Their lives always center around work and their children and other women (since a woman cannot have a man for a friend without the worst kind of ostracism and gossip). They indulge their husbands. . . . Prais[ing] their smallest accomplishments. . . . No wonder the men are childish. And a grown child is a dangerous thing, especially since, among the Olinka, the husband has life and death power over the wife. If he accuses one of his wives of witchcraft or infidelity, she can be killed. (P. 153)

Nettie's descriptions of the experiences of African women argue that Black women's oppression is transcultural. Celie's situation is then placed within a larger framework, linking her Black American experiences with those of Black women in Africa. In one letter, Nettie clearly makes that connection:

There is a way that the [Olinka] men speak to women that reminds me too much of Pa. They listen just long enough to issue instructions. They don't even look at women when women are speaking. They look at the ground and bend their heads toward the ground. The women also do not "look in a man's face," as they say. To "look in a man's face" is a brazen thing to do. They look instead at his feet or his knees. And what can I say to this? Again, it is our own behavior around Pa. (P. 14)

The two sets of letters—Nettie's narration of the Olinka experience and Celie's self-narration—intersect to map out Walker's womanist ideology. Both marginalize the historical discourse that would focus primarily on imperialism in Africa and racism in America in order to emphasize another "history": the story of the universal oppression of Black women. While the novel attempts closure with its representation of an economically and socially empowered Celie and its strong suggestion of reconciliation, its ideological project—the mapping out of "womanist" ideology—is strikingly highlighted. Celie and Nettie express the previously silenced voices of women such as Mem and Margaret. Moreover, the novel achieves its goals through the radical appropriation of the epistolary form and its deployment of images and representations that defamiliarize practices and conditions endemic to the oppression of women. Displacing a history that focuses on external racial conflict with a genealogy that inscribes a mode of feminist consciousness compels the reader to view those practices and conditions in a new light.

The Salt Eaters

Although critical studies of Toni Cade Bambara's *The Salt Eaters* have not totally ignored its feminist content, they have focused primarily on the structure of the novel and its cultural and historical references, connecting it to other discourses that attempt to reproduce Afro-American culture. Such approaches seem to avoid facing the complex issues generated by

the novel's representations of gender politics, subordinating
that concern to a racial discourse.

Arguing, for example, that *The Salt Eaters* is "long, intri-
cately written, trickily structured, full of learning, heavy with
wisdom," Gloria Hull advances one of the most lucid discussions of the novel's structure. Her approach to the novel, however, places it within the canonized texts of Afro-American
literature. Responding to what she views as the significance of
the novel, Hull writes:

It is a daringly brilliant work which accomplishes even better for the
1980s what *Native Son* did for the 1940s, *Invisible Man* for the 1950s,
or *Song of Solomon* for the 1970s; it fixes our present and challenges
the way to the future. Reading it deeply should result in personal
transformation; teaching it can be a political act.[14]

What is significantly omitted from Hull's discussion of the
novel is a context of feminist inscriptions or reference to any
women-centered texts. Hull articulates her position on the
feminist content of the novel when she observes that Bambara
is "*also* creating from her identity as a woman writer" (italics
added).[15] *The Salt Eaters*, according to this reading, is a complex cultural and political novel grounded in the ideology of
Black liberation; its feminist inscriptions are only secondary
considerations.

Eleanor Traylor, examining the novel as a "modern myth
of creation told in a jazz mode," provides a rich reading of its
themes and narrative structure, establishing a homology between its form and that of jazz compositions. In a celebratory
and dense reading, Traylor situates the novel within the broad
spectrum of Afro-American cultural practices. Identifying textual links and what might be viewed as semiotic redundan-
cies[16] between Bambara's novels and Afro-American music,
she argues:

The Salt Eaters, like one complex jazz symphony, orchestrates the
chordal riffs introduced in the short stories of Toni Cade Bambara.
. . . The improvising, stylizing, vamping, re-creative method of the

jazz composer is the formal method by which the narrative genius
of Toni Cade Bambara evokes a usable past testing its values within
an examined present moment while simultaneously exploring the re-
creative and transformative possibilities of experience. The method
of the jazz composition informs the central themes and larger revela-
tion of the world of Bambara's fiction.[17]

Traylor's highly provocative treatment of Bambara's narrative strategies offer the reader an exciting approach to the
novel. Nevertheless, as Hull privileges political content, Traylor's focus on the synthesis of form and content and its textual relationships carries strong ideological implications. In
her painstakingly detailed reading, Traylor pays little attention
to the feminist dimension of the novel. It is subsumed by the
celebration of Afro-American culture that her essay evokes.

Focusing on the language and the ideological issues related
to Black cultural nationalism in *The Salt Eaters*, Ruth Elizabeth Burks sees the work as inferior to Bambara's short stories,
as a significant failure in language and a loss of political vision.
Her response to the novel's apparently elliptical and disjointed
structure is to view it as an aesthetic disaster and the universe
it depicts as an epistemological failure. Burks writes:

The Salt Eaters is a novel—Bambara's first—and therefore immediately differentiated from her other works. Its language is the language
of the old, convoluted in its twists and turns, its sophistication,
its punctuation, and its highly imaginative tones. These characters
speak little, because they have lost the desire to communicate with
each other through words. Their thoughts, as conveyed by Bambara,
are more real to them than that which is real.[18]

Burks elaborates on her interpretation, applying it to her
reading of Velma's malaise. For Burks, the novel's protagonist
represents the epitome of the "failure of language to provoke
positive action," and the solution is quite simple:

She has to find the internal wholeness, the meeting ground between
words and actions that will allow her to positively affect her external surroundings. To accomplish this all she has to do is want to be

well and spiritually whole; then words and actions can assume their proper place. Velma must put off feeling sorry for herself and perceive that she is the instrument for her people, as are we all. Like Christ, she must die (at least symbolically) and live again to absolve herself and her people from their current sin of apathy. But, unlike Christ's, her metamorphosis into the world of the spirit derives its strength from her people: African people.[19]

This interesting but problematic reading of Velma's character raises serious questions. First, one must examine the assumptions that underpin it. Velma, according to Burks, must "want to be well and spiritually whole" in order "to positively affect her external surroundings." She must become a martyr—suggested by the references to symbolic death, absolution, and Christ—and find her strength in "her people: African people."

The argument that Velma's disintegration is generated by personal failure rejects some of the major ideological representations of the novel. The difficulties that Velma (and other women) experience with male dominance, the disjuncture between the myth of Black cultural nationalism and its efficacy as a political tool, and the tenuous grounds on which "the Black community" is constructed go unnoted by Burk. Her argument seems to ignore the feminist dimensions of the novel, proposing a reading largely influenced by the politics of cultural nationalism.

The constant that one might locate in all these readings is the desire for a single, coherent voice. Each critic's interpretive strategy resists the apparent epistemological disorder that pervades the novel and retrieves a single unifying element. Bambara's enunciation of her ideology in *The Salt Eaters* would seem to encourage such readings, suggesting that it focuses on a central unifying problem. While she was still in the process of completing the novel, Bambara voiced her central concern:

I gave myself an assignment based on observation: there is a split between the spiritual, psychic, and political forces in my community. Not since the maroon experience of Toussaint's era have psychic technicians and spiritual folk (medicine people) and guerrillas (warriors) merged. It is a wasteful and dangerous split. The novel grew out of my attempt to fuse the seemingly separate frames of references of the camps; it grew out of an interest in identifying bridges; it grew out of a compulsion to understand how the energies of this period will manifest themselves in the next decade.[20]

The repetition of her position reinforces its centrality to the ideological project of the novel. The Seven Sisters' assertion that "the material without the spiritual and psychic does not a dialectic make"[21] and Sophie Heywood's that "there was a Babel of paths, of plans" because a "deep rift had been developing . . . beginning with the move toward the material world and away from nature" are fictional references to Bambara's argument. The need for synthesis is argued even further as the novel presents Campbell's arrival at a state of heightened consciousness:

What came to Campbell . . . was a flash in the brain pan, and he knew he'd struck gold. Knew in a glowing moment that all the systems were the same at base—voodoo, thermodynamics, I Ching, astrology, numerology, alchemy, metaphysics, everybody's ancient myth—they are interchangeable, not at all separate, much less conflicting. They were the same, to the extent that their origins survived detractors and perverters. How simple universal knowledge is after all, he grinned. (P. 210)

The processing of a discourse that fuses the "material and the spiritual," then, apparently constitutes the major textual focus of *The Salt Eaters*. I would argue, however, that the narrative's form and its representational strategies generate additional issues that open the novel to alternative readings. The metaphorical emplotment and the intensification of schizophrenia as a textual dominant, as well as the substantive rewriting of the feminist discourse of Bambara's short stories, are prime factors in the novel's production of ideology.

In order to come to terms with the novel's discontinuities, radical alterations of spatial and temporal relationships, and moments of self-deconstruction, a broader understanding of the inscription and production of schizophrenic discourse in the text is necessary. Although I have used the term *schizophrenia* to denote the collision of two ideological discourses—the racially grounded one and one informed by gender politics—such an understanding only partially addresses the narrative's complexities. Fredric Jameson's appropriation of Lacan to read schizophrenia as one of the "basic features of postmodernism" can provide a useful framework in which to rethink the concept of the schizophrenic text. Paraphrasing Lacan, Jameson argues that two aspects of the schizophrenic, both brought about by language, are the disintegration of temporal continuity and "an experience of isolated, disconnected, discontinuous material signifiers that fail to link up into a coherent sequence."[22]

Applying this reading of schizophrenia to *The Salt Eaters* means modifying it somewhat. Temporal discontinuities and "isolated, disconnected discontinuous, material signifiers" are inscribed within the text. Consequently, one might argue that it possesses an apparent anomie, as if it were the product of an anomic consciousness. Yet this fragmented and schizophrenic textual construction is essential to the novel's production of ideology. *The Salt Eaters* can be read as a novel in which an ideological position marked by concern for the social and political disintegration of an organic Black community is intensified and reinforced by a seeming disintegration of the narrative.

The Salt Eaters most dramatically displays its schizophrenic character in its treatment of time. The overlapping of present and future time and the reification of the past result in time presented as a series of images read in the context of a present crisis and contribute to the dissonance and an atmosphere of tension. Contained in time constructs of past, present, and future is a heteroglossia of voices, each addressing some aspect of the ideological crisis that the novel represents. This textual strategy suggests Bakhtin's comments on the polyphonic structuring of the novel:

The decentralizing of the verbal–ideological world that finds its expression in the novel begins by presuming fundamentally differentiate social groups, which exist in an intense and vital interaction with other social groups. A sealed-off interest group, caste or class, existing within an internally unitary and unchanging core of its own, cannot serve as socially productive soil for the development of the novel unless it becomes riddled with decay or shifted somehow from its state of internal balance and self-sufficiency.[23]

What one observes in *The Salt Eaters*, then, is a far more complex narration than is found in Bambara's short fiction. Both *Gorilla* and *Seabirds*, because of their commitment to an ideological discourse of cultural nationalism, largely assume a narrative mode that is wedded to classic realism and characterized by monologue. The focus is on an organic, somewhat nonproblematic Black community. Hence, the stories appear to be unified, coherent discourse engaged in either celebrating that community or representing its conflicts with a hostile Other. By contrast, in *The Salt Eaters* that community is the site of uncertainty and disintegration where heterogeneous, as well as dissonant and contradictory, desires surface. This paradoxical aspect of the novel manifests itself in the fusion of dystopian and utopian visions, its deconstruction and reconstruction of the immediate historical past, and its questioning and subverting of its own enterprise.

The utopian construct that constitutes a trajectory of desire is the material–spiritual synthesis earlier discussed by Bambara. It is reiterated in the novel through observations made by Campbell and the Seven Sisters. In *The Salt Eaters*, this utopia is presented as accessible and partially realized. The deference that the medical community gives to Minnie Ransom in her role as faith healer—an issue I treat more extensively later in this chapter—the Academy as the site at which "teachers

. . . were steadily realigning cultural and political loyalties" (p. 167), and the representation of the Seven Sisters as projections of possible "Third World" or "women-of-color" unity all encode a possible realization and activation of the utopian project.

Nevertheless, coexisting with this utopian promise is a social milieu that narrates a counterreality, a vision that approaches the apocalyptic. The "real" present is marked by moral disintegration and political impotence in the community, by the threat of nuclear disaster represented by Transchemical, and, above all, by the tensions between men and women. Present time, then, which can be said both to embody and to project the future, also stands as its antithesis. The juxtaposition of the two modalities and the largely fragmentary and elliptical construction of the utopian future produce narrative fragmentation. In the process of producing a utopian vision, the novel creates within the same space a dystopian present, sometimes resulting in an overlapping of the two.

Present time is also the vehicle through which the past is evoked and read. While the narration of past history is sometimes a textual strategy that permits the illumination of particular characters (e.g., Old Wife and Minnie and the friendship between Fred Holt and Porter), it is often encoded in episodic moments and isolated but sharply focused images that contain critiques and deconstructions of the historical moment.

In Bambara's collections of short stories, racial strife is simply represented as an inner world (Black)/outer world (white) opposition. Critiquing political movements in general or Blacks in particular is omitted from the texts. *The Salt Eaters* views racial conflict from a different angle. The reconstruction of the past raises issues about male participation and performance in liberation struggles and places male and female differences in the foreground. A single image might disrupt and subvert what appears to be a straightforward narration. This narrative strategy is particularly effective in the juxtaposition of two images when Velma evokes her past to recall her involvement in political activism. Both images inscribe representations of the body in an arena of strife. The first is focused on Velma, who in the process of a political demonstration experiences menstruation and is forced to address her condition while "mount[ing] a raggedy tampon . . . in a nasty bathroom with no stall doors" in a Gulf station that she and her group are boycotting. Although physically and verbally assaulted, she continues to march, with swollen feet and "reeking of wasted blood and rage."

In direct contrast, "the speaker" arrives escorted by "eye-stinging shiny, black sleek limousines" and proceeds to perform: "He looked a bit like King, had a delivery similar to Malcolm's, dressed like Stokely, had glasses like Rap, but she'd never heard him say anything useful or offensive. But what a voice. And what a good press agent. And the people had bought him. What a disaster. But what a voice" (p. 35).

Immediately after this parody of a speaker/leader, the novel returns to Velma's ordeal in the bathroom: "And no soap. No towels. No tissue. No machine. Just a spurt then a trickle of rusty water in the clogged sink then no water at all. And like a cat she'd had to lick herself clean of grit, salt, blood, and rage" (p. 36).

The juxtaposition of the two images not only demythologizes the male figure, but shows Velma to be heroic and the person with true political commitment. The male body is presented as an aggregate of signifiers that suggest superficiality rather than substance. The metaphorical references to "a delivery similar to Malcolm's," "dressed like Stokely," and "glasses like Rap" parody the misperception of style for substance that often characterized Black "leaders" in the 1960s. The nameless leader/speaker becomes the embodiment of the myth of Black militancy, a myth undermined and subverted through parody. This subversion of the myth is further reinforced by the novel's insertion of Velma's humiliating experience.

This demythologizing of the male leadership figure is ad-

dressed again when the women accuse the men of "operating
. . . a social club" and "renting limousines and profiling in
your three-piece suits and imported pajamas while the people
sweat it out through hard times" (p. 37). The women's rebellion leads to autonomy and the formation of a group called
Women for Action.

The critique of the past that reads male dominance and
duplicity as aspects of traditional nationalist politics becomes
an ideologeme of the broader feminist discourse of the novel.
Velma's madness, the power and influence of Minnie Ransom,
a distinct community of women and girls, and the dangers
posed by Black men who prey on the women of the community clearly focus on problems of Black women's empowerment
within their communities.

"Velma Henry" serves a dual function as character and sign
in the novel. Her disintegration and fragmentation reflect the
"madness" of the community as a whole, and her attempt to
move from illness to health (fragmentation to wholeness) represents both a personal process and one in which the larger
community is engaged. Her character, then, assumes a complex representational status. In addition to an individual, personal narrative, Velma Henry is a metaphor for a larger story
that the novel addresses: the dissonance and discord, discontinuities and rupture, of the Black community. The inscription
of personal schizophrenia becomes dialectically related to the
social disintegration of the community, and the relationship
between the two is sustained by the novel's employing a form
that reproduces that disorder. Nevertheless, it is in the specific exploration of Velma's ordeal that the novel processes its
feminist discourse.

What one sees in the character of Velma is a subversion of representations in Bambara's earlier fiction (particularly in *Seabirds*) of the commitment of Black women to the
largely male-defined political struggles of their communities.
Although women such as Virginia in "The Organizer's Wife,"
Lacey in "Broken Field Running," and Naomi in "The Ap-

prentice" all react with ambivalence to the demands made on them, they still sacrifice personal desires for those of "the struggle." This suppression of the personal becomes a necessary condition for involvement in nationalist politics, and despite doubts and uneasiness, the women invariably reconcile their personal goals with those of the larger political project.

Velma's collapse can be read as a serious questioning of the wisdom of self-negation in the interest of a totalizing ideology and a rebellion against it. Confronted with the demands and contradictions of the movement in the public arena and the discord in her marriage to Obie at the personal level, Velma is driven to madness and attempted suicide. The textual inscription of her "illness," however, is ambiguous. Whether functioning as a sign of being overwhelmed by forces in the community or in her private life, Velma's attempted suicide can be read as an act of rebellion against the injustices experienced by her and other women, an act that allows her to reexamine and reconstruct her life. Sophie Heywood's observation, as reflected by the narrator, that "[m]aybe the act of trying to sever a vein or climbing into the oven was like going to the caves, a beginning" (p. 148) strongly supports this interpretation.

For Velma, that beginning consists of evoking images of the past and understanding how that past contributed to her present crisis. In the long interior monologue in which she reflects on how "she might have died" (pp. 271–276), she comes to grips with the internal and external threats to her existence and the strength that she derived from "M'Dear Sophie's" support. This examination of the past, central to Velma's healing process, leads her to realize that "the hunt for balance and kinship was the thing. A mutual courtesy. She would run to the park and hunt for self. Would be wild. Would look" (p. 267).

This emphasis on "mutual courtesy," self-discovery, and wildness distinguishes Velma from the women in the earlier stories and contributes to the overall feminist aspect of the novel. While the political needs of the community are still represented and addressed, the issues of desire and the empowerment of Black women in the community are consistently in the foreground.

The novel's feminist discourse is further developed through its depiction of Minnie Ransom, "the fabled faith healer of the district." Even her mode of attire—the dress made of kenti cloth, the *gelee*, a specifically African headwear popular among Black women who identify with cultural nationalism—semiotically addresses her cultural and political significance. She is the embodiment of Black women's culture. In the following passage, Nadeen, observing Minnie's healing of Velma, points out Minnie's cultural significance:

This was what it was supposed to be. . . . People standing about wishing Mrs. Henry well and knowing Miss Ransom would do what she said she would do. Miss Ransom know to calm fretful babies with a smile or a pinch of the thigh, know to cool out nervous wives who bled all the time and couldn't stand still, know to dissolve hard lumps in the body that the doctors at the hospital called cancers. This was the real thing. Miss Ransom in her flouncy dress and hip shoes with flowers peeking out of her turban and smelling like coconut Afro spray. Even Cousin Dorcas, who had gone to specialists as far away as Boston, said this was the real place and Miss Ransom was the real thing. (P. 113)

Minnie Ransom's role in the Southwest Community Infirmary might be read as the material–spiritual synthesis the novel addresses. Significantly, however, Minnie represents a triumph of folk wisdom over scientific knowledge, of women's culture over patriarchal dominance. She symbolizes the valorization of a specific Black women's culture that one sees in the works of many Black women writers, among them Alice Walker, Paule Marshall, Toni Morrison, and Gloria Naylor. Race and gender specific, this culture, embodied in *The Salt Eaters* by Minnie Ransom, becomes both an assertion of difference and a mode of opposition. This celebration of an alternative culture, however, has resemblances to similar constructions in all radical feminist discourses.[24]

The Salt Eaters further develops its feminist ideology

through its representation of the cohesiveness of women's communities. The bonds between Old Wife and Minnie and Sophie and Velma are replicated throughout the novel by similar relationships, for example, those of Nadeen, for whom Velma's healing becomes a rite of passage, and the Seven Sisters, who represent a projected political goal.

Nadeen's initiation into womanhood and a community of Black women occurs when she experiences in Velma's healing "a kinship with the woman she did not even know," which enables her to transcend her devalued status and affirm an identity:

Nadeen knew she was not the stupid girl her teachers thought she was, or the silly child the nurses thought she was. . . . She could argue now with folks at the clinic. How come she was old enough to sign the papers giving consent for the baby to be taken care of when it came, but wasn't old enough to sign for herself, had to have her aunt and the social worker give consent? It was always the same— too old to do this, too young to do that. No more. Nadeen moved closer and would have moved right up to the two stools to join hands with the healer and the woman, if the prayer group weren't there around the two like a gate. She was a woman. Or at least . . . she was womanish. (P. 106)

Although Nadeen further develops the feminist project of the novel by representing the powers of transformation that exist in women's communities, the Seven Sisters represent a possible future community. Central to their representation is a desire for a multiethnic sisterhood that is unified in its stance against racial and patriarchal dominance.[25] The political vision embraces the ideological concept of "women-of-color." Because it represents that which is yet to be realized, its inscription in the novel is somewhat fragmentary. The women, united by their commitment to political and cultural activism, create a sense of community through the sharing of the stories of their lives. But a coherent ideological position is depicted as more "in process" than actually realized.[26]

The feminist discourse of *The Salt Eaters* is reinforced by the novel's depiction of males. The several male figures presented in the text—the ambiguous characterization of Meadows, the sympathetic portrayals of Fred Holt and Porter, the possibility of transformation in Obie, and the idealized representation of Campbell—argue against reading the novel as a total rejection of Black males. Yet it inscribes, in far more graphic terms than any of Bambara's earlier works, the image of some Black males as nonproductive and destructive forces in their communities. I addressed this earlier in my discussion of the deconstruction of the myth of male leadership by the Women of Action. Depictions of the "boymen" and of Roland as rapist are even more radical textualizations of the threat to women represented by some men in the community.

The boymen, also described as the "welfare men" and "half men," represent the decay and disintegration of the community. The text emphasizes their intimidation and exploitation of the women of the community. Seen through the eyes of Meadows, the narrative presents an unsavory and depressing portrait of the boymen:

He had seen them, made a study of them, knew the look, the posture. In parks, on roofs, in bars, on stoops, but especially in the supermarket running their whining line while the women reached round them for a can of whatever was on sale. The boymen grabbing at their pocketbooks or their arms and the women saying "Naw, man, gotta feed my kids." Then the whine heard all over the market and the women mashing the can against the shelf for two cents off for dents. "But mamma, look here" or "Say Baby I gotta" and then the "Naaaw man." But never a name, never names. A ritual. Market theater with anonymous personae. . . .
And the women, defeated, would dip into the coins and give it up, then look over the items moving along on the belt for the one thing the children might possibly do without. (Pp. 182–183)

This depiction of the boymen as predators recalls the earlier representation of Roland, Obie's brother, as rapist. In both instances, the males, in pursuit of their own gratification, dehumanize the women of the community. In a narrative strategy that allows the reader to witness and experience Roland's act, the novel presents it through the combined perspectives of Obie and Roland:

They got me up here mopping floors, bro. She'd been mopping up her own blood with the mop Roland had threatened her with, taken from her, and hit her with, surprising her from the garage window. Mopping up her own blood when the police arrived. A Black woman, forty-six years old, four children, her husband in the reserves for nine days. Roland climbing in the window, stepping over bikes, skateboards, stacks of comics, a burnt-out TV. She'd been in the kitchen mopping the floor. Roland had sent him the newspaper clippings. *Awwwww shit man, ain't like she was a virgin.* Obie had flown up for the trial. *Shit, she was probably on the pill.* And he had studied them both. Roland, hard mouth and surly, his head dropped to the side bobbing like the hydrophobic patient he'd helped Doc Serge get to the hospital three summers before. *Don't cry, bitch, or I'll really hurt you.* The woman huddled on the stand, pinched, nasal, but determined to get justice. *Be good to me, ain't nobody been good to me.* She might have been their Aunt Frances, an older sister. She was. *Be sweet now and I'll be gone fore your children get back.* (Pp. 96–97)

Departing from the dominant text, the material–spiritual synthesis, these two episodes represent the dystopic vision in the narrative. More important, they specifically address the vulnerability of women in the community. In Bambara's earlier works, particularly *Seabirds*, terror was seen as coming from without, and the community was a refuge or sanctuary. Trans-chemical symbolizes that "outside" threat in *The Salt Eaters*, but an additional threat against women is seen as emanating from forces within the community.

Bambara's ideological call for synthesis and the creation of a new political vision is arguably dominant in the narrative. Within that project, however, is a strong assertion of feminist desire. Velma's "madness," Minnie's subversion of the scientific and patriarchal, and the celebration of an image of united womanhood herald the eruption of feminist consciousness. The criticism directed against the boymen and Roland further position that consciousness of the oppression of women over any romantic representation of an idyllic community. Thus the novel marks a radical departure from Bambara's earlier works. The apparent narrative dissonances and discontinuities, the fragmentary inscription of episodes, and the seemingly arbitrary shifting of narrative consciousness are all signs of a Black feminist ideological position in process.

New Forms and Strategies

The narrations and representational strategies in *Tar Baby*, *The Color Purple*, and *The Salt Eaters* suggest major revisions and rewritings of earlier works by Morrison, Walker, and Bambara. The problems of place, or community, in Morrison's novel; the radical experimentation with the epistolary form and the empowerment of a disempowered female in *The Color Purple*; and Bambara's "schizophrenia," characterized by a fusion of the dystopic and utopian and reinforced by the eruption of feminist desire—all indicate the surfacing of a new consciousness. In these textual strategies, the novels are somewhat similar to Jacques Derrida's category of texts that "operate breaches or infractions at the most advanced level."

Certain texts . . . seemed to me to mark and to organize a structure of resistance to the philosophical conceptuality that allegedly dominated or comprehended them, whether directly or whether through categories derived from their philosophical fund, the categories of esthetics, rhetoric, or traditional criticism. For example, the values of meaning or of content, of form, or signifier, of metaphor/metonomy, of truth, of representation, etc. . . . can no longer account for certain determined effects of these texts.[27]

The modes of narration in these recent works of Bambara, Morrison, and Walker may be said to represent such breaches or infractions. Not only do they radically break with textual strategies in the writers' earlier fiction, but (particularly in Walker and Bambara) they seem to subvert our traditional expectations of the novel. The strategies employed and narratives produced are suggestive of Raymond Williams's concept of a structure of feeling—"a kind of feeling and thinking which is indeed social and material, but each in an embryonic phase before it can become fully articulate and defined exchange,"[28]—that signifies the emergence of a specific Black feminist consciousness.

In a brilliant afterword to her edited collection of essays on the literary practices of Black women, Hortense Spillers addresses the issue of the relationship of form and content in the writings of Afro-American women. Using a Foucauldian model of "archaeology of narrative strategies," she situates Black women's literary tradition within a social and historical context:

I would claim for black women writers the widest possible application of the term [tradition] at the same time that I would employ it as a working word to differentiate the literature that speaks to a particular historical order as counter-tradition, a counter-myth. . . . would want to say that "tradition" for black women's writing community is a matrix of literary discontinuities that partially articulate various periods of consciousness of the African-American people.[29]

I have focused on specific periods of consciousness of three Afro-American women writers and have explored the relationship of a politics of race and gender to the narrative strategies and production of ideology in their works. In doing so, I have attempted to explore the intricacies and complexities that characterize a race- and gender-specific literature in which narrative is the locus of contending desires and a significant textual event: the self-representation and construction of the Black female subject and the processing of Black feminist desire.

NOTES

BIBLIOGRAPHY

INDEX

Notes

INTRODUCTION

1. Peter Brooks, *Reading for the Plot: Design and Intention in Narrative* (New York: Vintage, 1985), 38, 39. Hereafter cited in the text by page number.

2. One of the major difficulties I find in his typology is Brooks's distinction between male and female plots. If one's grasp of this concept depends on the examples provided, one would conclude that the male plot involves a male protagonist, while the female plot places a female in the foreground. This, it seems to me, is somewhat reductionist, but the issue is beyond the scope of the present study.

3. Catherine Belsey, *Critical Practice* (London: Methuen, 1980), 85.

4. Julia Kristeva, *Desire in Language: A Semiotic Approach to Literature and Art*, ed. Leon S. Roudiez and trans. Thomas Zora, Alice Jardine, and Leon S. Roudiez (New York: Columbia University Press, 1980), 111.

5. Dominick LaCapra, *Rethinking Intellectual History: Texts, Contexts, Language* (Ithaca: Cornell University Press, 1983), 36.

6. Toni Morrison, "Rootedness: The Ancestor as Foundation," in *Black Women Writers (1950–1980): A Critical Evaluation*, ed. Mari Evans (Garden City, N.Y.: Doubleday Anchor, 1984), 340. Hereafter cited in the text by page number.

7. Thomas Le Clair, "A Conversation with Toni Morrison: The Language Must Not Sweat," *New Republic* 184 (March 21, 1981): 25–29.

8. Morrison, "Rootedness," 341.

9. Claudia Tate, ed., *Black Women Writers at Work* (New York: Continuum, 1983), 122, 123.

10. For a discussion of Morrison's position and that of other Black feminists who were uncomfortable with the direction of liberal

feminism, see "The Women's Movement and Black Discontent," in Paula Giddings, *When and Where I Enter: The Impact of Black Women on Race and Sex in America* (New York: Bantam, 1985), 299–324. See also Chapter Two of this book.

11. Morrison, "Rootedness," 344.
12. Tate, *Black Women Writers at Work*, 17.
13. Toni Cade Bambara, "Salvation Is the Issue," in Evans, *Black Women Writers*, 47.
14. Preface to Toni Cade Bambara, ed., *The Black Woman: An Anthology* (New York: Signet, 1970), 8.
15. Toni Cade Bambara, "On the Issue of Roles," in ibid., 101.
16. Alice Walker, *In Search of Our Mothers' Gardens: Womanist Prose* (New York: Harcourt Brace Jovanovich, 1983), xi–xii. Hereafter cited in the text by page number.
17. In Chapter Five I explore this construction in more detail. The basic issue I raise is this: While the color symbolism involved in the analogy would justify its reading as a celebration of lesbianism, the definition remains ambiguous.
18. Tate, *Black Women Writers at Work*, 181.
19. Raymond Williams, *Marxism and Literature* (Oxford: Oxford University Press, 1977), 55.
20. See Louis Althusser, *Lenin and Philosophy and Other Essays*, trans. Ben Brewster (New York: Monthly Review Press, 1971), 162.
21. Raymond Williams, *Problems in Materialism and Culture* (London: Verso, 1980), 41.
22. See Annette Kuhn, *Women's Pictures: Feminism and Cinema* (London: Routledge and Kegan Paul, 1982), 3–18.
23. Linda Gordon, "What's New in Women's History," in *Feminist Studies/Critical Studies*, ed. Teresa de Lauretis (Bloomington: Indiana University Press, 1986), 30.
24. See Fredric Jameson, "Metacommentary," in *Contemporary Literary Criticism: Modernism Through Post-Structuralism*, ed. Robert Con Davis (New York: Longman, 1986), 112.

CHAPTER ONE

1. See Houston A. Baker, Jr., *Blues, Ideology, and Afro-American Literature: A Vernacular Theory* (Chicago: University of Chicago Press, 1984), 72–91.

2. M. M. Bahktin and P. M. Medvedev, *The Formal Method in Literary Scholarship: A Critical Introduction to Sociological Poetics*, trans. Albert J. Wherle (Cambridge: Harvard University Press, 1985), 14.

3. Charles V. Hamilton, "Riots, Revolts, and Relevant Responses," in *The Black Power Revolt: A Collection of Essays*, ed. Floyd B. Barbour (Boston: Porter Sargent, 1968), 175.

4. While this essay focuses on Black Aesthetic discourse as it relates to literary production, there are interesting studies of its impact on other cultural and artistic practices. In "Black Power and the American Christ" (Barbour, *Black Power Revolt*, 85–93), Vincent Harding discusses the ideological need to transform the symbolism of traditional Christian practices in order to make it more compatible with the doctrine of Black Power, and Murry DePillars, in his important essay "The Emerging Voice of the Black Visual Artist" (*Black Art: An International Quarterly* 1, no. 1 [1976]: 50–52), calls on Black painters to create images of and for themselves.

5. Alvin F. Pouissant, "The Negro American: His Self Image and Integration," in Barbour, *Black Power Revolt*, 101.

6. See Irene Portis Winner, "Ethnicity, Modernity, and Theory of Culture Texts," in *The Semiotics of Culture*, ed. Irene Portis Winner and Jean Umiker-Sebeok (The Hague: Mouton, 1979), 103–147.

7. See Stephen Greenblatt, *Renaissance Self-Fashioning: From More to Shakespeare* (Chicago: University of Chicago Press, 1980), 3.

8. See Richard Wright, "Blueprint for Negro Literature," in *Richard Wright Reader*, ed. Ellen Wright and Michel Fabre (New York: Harper & Row, 1978). Hereafter cited in the text by page number.

9. See Barbara A. Babcock, "Introduction," in her *The Reversible World: Symbolic Inversion in Art and Society* (Ithaca: Cornell University Press, 1978), 14.

10. See V. N. Voloshinov [M. M. Bakhtin?], *Marxism and the Philosophy of Language*, trans. L. Matejka and I. R. Titunik (New York and London: Seminar Press, 1973), 23.

11. See Hoyt W. Fuller, "Towards A Black Aesthetic," in *The Black Aesthetic*, ed. Addison Gayle, Jr. (New York: Doubleday Anchor, 1972), 3.

12. Gayle, *Black Aesthetic*, 40.

13. Larry Neal, "The Black Arts Movement," *Drama Review* 12, no. 4 (Summer 1968): 29.

14. Cesaire argued that the concept of Negritude, generated by Black cultural nationalism in the 1930s, was even more relevant in the 1960s, a time of revolutionary political change. See William Robinson, ed., *Nomma* (New York: Macmillan, 1972), 230–237. Much to the chagrin of some nationalists of the period, Frantz Fanon argued against what he viewed as a simplistic and reductionist equating of the political situations and cultures of Africans and Afro-Americans.

15. See Larry Neal, "And Shine Swam On: An Afterword," in *Black Fire: An Anthology of Afro-American Writing*, ed. LeRoi Jones and Larry Neal (New York: Morrow, 1968), 653.

16. Maulana Ron Karenga, "Black Cultural Nationalism," in Gayle, *Black Aesthetic*, 32.

17. Jones and Neal, *Black Fire*, 655.

18. Ibid.

19. Neal, "Black Arts Movement," 39.

20. The elaborate theorizing of Althusser on the workings of ideology is particularly relevant here. See Louis Althusser, *Lenin and Philosophy and Other Essays*, trans. Ben Brewster (New York: Monthly Review Press, 1971), 127–186. His argument that ideology constructs subjectivity through a "representation of the imaginary relationship of individuals to their real conditions of their existence," while focused on the relationship between hegemonic and subordinate groups, might be applied to alternative formations such as Black Aesthetic discourse. The Black Aestheticians, like Wright before them, viewed as their primary mission the reproduction of the lived experiences of the Black masses in artistic narratives, with a goal of developing heightened political consciousness.

21. See Manning Marable, *How Capitalism Underdeveloped Black America: Problems in Race, Political Economy, and Society* (Boston: South End Press, 1983).

22. Larry Neal, "Four Our Women," in Jones and Neal, *Black Fire*, 320.

23. Neal, "Black Arts Movement," 38; Greenblatt, *Renaissance Self-Fashioning*, 228.

CHAPTER TWO

1. Barbara Smith, "Toward A Black Feminist Criticism," in *But Some of Us Are Brave: Black Women's Studies*, ed. Gloria T. Hull, Patricia Bell Scott, and Barbara Smith (New York: Feminist Press, 1983), 159.

2. For a discussion of the roles assigned to Black women in the Black political movement and the white feminist movement, see Marable, *How Capitalism Underdeveloped Black America*; and Paula Giddings, *When and Where I Enter: The Impact of Black Women on Race and Sex in America* (New York: Bantam, 1985), 299–324.

3. See "The Combahee River Collective: A Black Feminist Statement," in *Capitalist Patriarchy and the Case for Socialist Feminism*, ed. Zillah R. Eisenstein (New York: Monthly Review Press, 1979), 363. Hereafter cited in the text by page number.

4. Lucien Goldmann, *Towards A Sociology of the Novel*, trans. Alan Sheridan (London: Tavistock, 1978), 156.

5. Ibid., 158.

6. Sandra M. Gilbert and Susan Gubar, *The Madwoman in the Attic: The Woman Writer and the Nineteenth-Century Literary Imagination* (New Haven: Yale University Press, 1979), 49.

7. Ibid.

8. Hazel V. Carby, *Reconstructing Womanhood: The Emergence of the Afro-American Woman Novelist* (New York: Oxford University Press, 1987), 16.

9. My concepts of "inner" and "outer" worlds are adapted from Lotman. According to Ann Shukman's reading of Lotman, "The inner/outer opposition may be variously interpreted in dif-

ferent cultures and different texts as 'own people/other people,' 'believers/heathens,' 'culture/barbarity.' " Of course, implicit in my reading of Hurston's works is the concept of an imaginary (i.e., created by images) inner world of Black women that posits its opposition to outer worlds of white men and women and Black men. See Ann Shukman, *Literature and Semiotics: A Study of the Writings of Yu. M. Lotman* (Amsterdam: North-Holland, 1977), 95–96.

10. Michel Foucault, *Power/Knowledge: Selected Interviews and Other Writings 1972–77*, ed. Colin Gordon and trans. Colin Gordon, Leo Marshall, John Mepham, and Kate Soper (New York: Pantheon, 1980), 82. Examining Hurston's works within this framework were first made possible by my discussions with Harryette Mullen, who viewed the lying sessions in *Mules and Men* as examples of Hurston's valorizing subjugated knowledges. I have attempted here to expand on Mullen's insight, applying it to other aspects of Hurston's narrative strategy.

11. See "From the Natives' Point of View: On the Nature of Anthropological Understanding," in Clifford Geertz, *Local Knowledge: Further Essays in Interpretive Anthropology* (New York: Basic Books, 1983), 55–70. Adapting the terms "experience-near" and "experience-distant" from the psychoanalyst Heinz Kohut, Geertz defines the former term to indicate what a person "might himself naturally and effortlessly use to define what he or his fellows see, feel, think, imagine, and so on, and which he would readily understand when applied to by others." An "experience-distant" concept is described by Geertz as one that "specialists . . . employ to forward their scientific, philosophical, or practical aims."

12. See Barbara Johnson, "Thresholds of Difference: Structures of Address in Zora Neale Hurston," *Critical Inquiry* 12, no. 1 (Autumn 1985): 278–289.

13. Ibid., 286.

14. The phrase "literary mode of production" is from Terry Eagleton, who describes it as "a unity of certain forces and social relations of literary production in a social formation." See Terry Eagleton, *Criticism and Ideology: A Study in Marxist Literary Theory* (London: Verso Press, 1982), 45.

15. See Arna Bontemps, *Black Thunder: Gabriel's Revolt: Virginia: 1800* (Boston: Beacon Press, 1968; originally published by Macmillan in 1936).

16. See William Attaway, *Let Me Breathe Thunder* (New York: Doubleday, 1939), and *Blood on the Forge* (New York: Doubleday, 1941).

17. Basil Bernstein, "Social Class, Language, and Socialisation" in *Power and Ideology in Education*, ed. Jerome Karabel and A. H. Halsey (New York: Oxford University Press, 1977).

18. Zora Neale Hurston, *Their Eyes Were Watching God* (Urbana: University of Illinois Press, 1978; originally published by Lippincott in 1937), 29. Hereafter cited in the text by page number.

19. What I have in mind here is analogous to Lacan's *point de capiton*, or "primal metaphor." For Lacan, such a signifier ends the "process of transposition *(glissement)* of "ambulatory" signifieds in a discourse, pinning them down and producing a new signification. See Anthony Wilden, "Lacan and the Discourse of the Other," in Jacques Lacan, *Speech and Language in Psychoanalysis*, trans. Anthony Wilden (Baltimore: Johns Hopkins University Press, 1981), 274.

20. For a discussion of the controversy centered on this play and the impact it had on the personal and professional relationship of Hughes and Hurston, see Robert Hemenway, *Zora Neale Hurston: A Literary Biography* (Urbana: University of Illinois Press, 1977), 135–158.

21. For a discussion of *Eyes* as a revision of the tragic mulatta myth, see Barbara Christian, *Black Women Novelists: The Development of a Tradition, 1892–1976* (Westport, Conn.: Greenwood, 1980), 57–61.

CHAPTER THREE

1. See, for example, Dorothy H. Lee, "The Quest for Self: Triumph and Failure in the Works of Toni Morrison," and Darwin T. Turner, "Theme, Characterization in the Works of Toni Morrison," both in Evans, *Black Women Writers*, 346–360 and 361–369; Jane S. Braverman, "Failures of Love: Female Initiation

in the Novels of Toni Morrison," *American Literature* 52, no. 4 (January 1981): 541–563; Cynthia A. Davis, "Self, Society, and Myth in Toni Morrison's Fiction," *Contemporary Literature* 23, no. 3 (Summer 1982): 323–341; Bonnie Shipman Lane, "Toni Morrison's Rainbow Code," *Critique: Studies in Modern Fiction* 24, no. 3 (Spring 1983): 173–181; Jacqueline De Weever, "The Inverted World of Toni Morrison's *The Bluest Eye* and *Sula*," *College Language Association Journal* 22, no. 4 (June 1979): 402–414; and Grace Ann Hovet and Barbara Lounsberry, "Flying as Symbol and Legend in Toni Morrison's *The Bluest Eye, Sula*, and *Song of Solomon*," *College Language Association Journal* 27, no. 2 (December 1983): 119–140.

2. See Christian, *Black Women Novelists*. Hereafter cited in the text as *BWN* and followed by page number.

3. See Barbara Christian, "Community and Nature: The Novels of Toni Morrison" and "The Concept of Class in the Novels of Toni Morrison," both in Barbara Christian, *Black Feminist Criticism; Perspectives on Black Women Writers* (New York: Pergamon Press, 1985), 47–63 and 71–80. Hereafter cited in the text as *BFC* and followed by page number(s).

4. The difficulty a reader might encounter in attempting to follow Christian's argument is that *nature* is used to designate both patterns of conducts (or what might be called particular epistemologies or belief systems) and life styles, as well as forces outside human control. In a sense, her "problem" here reflects rather dramatically Raymond Williams's observation: "Nature is perhaps the most complex word in the language. It is relatively easy to distinguish three areas of meaning: (i) the essential quality and character of something; (ii) the inherent force which directs either the world or human beings or both; (iii) the material world itself, taken as including or not including human beings. Yet it is evident that within (ii) and (iii), though the area of reference is broadly clear, precise meanings are variable and at times even opposed." See Raymond Williams, *Keywords: A Vocabulary of Culture and Society*, rev. ed. (New York: Oxford University Press, 1983).

5. My reference to "a textual dominant" is a modification of Roman Jakobson's concept of the dominant as "the focusing component

of a work of art . . . [that] rules, determines and transforms the other components." For a discussion of Jakobson's concept, see Roman Jakobson, "The Dominant," in *Readings in Russian Poetics: Formalist and Structuralist Views*, ed. Ladislav Matejka and Krystyna Pomorska (Cambridge: MIT Press, 1971), 82–87.

6. See James H. Kavanagh, "To the Same Defect: Toward a Critique of the Ideology of the Aesthetic," *Bucknell Review* 29, no. 1 (1982): 104–105.

7. See Morrison, "Rootedness," 339–345; Nellie McKay, "An Interview with Toni Morrison," *Contemporary Literature* 24, no. 4 (Winter 1983): 413–429; Jane Bakerman, "The Seams Can't Show: An Interview with Toni Morrison," *Black American Literature Forum* 12 (1979): 56–60; Robert B. Stepto, "Intimate Things in Place: A Conversation with Toni Morrison," in *Chant of Saints: A Gathering of Afro-American Literature, Art, and Scholarship*, ed. Michael S. Harper and Robert B. Stepto (Urbana: University of Illinois Press, 1979), 213–229; and Tate, *Black Women Writers*, 117–131.

8. Much critical discussion of Morrison's novels has focused on an attempt to locate them within a specific genre. Because they generally combine realism with surrealism, attempts are sometimes made to designate them "magic realism." My position is that the larger ideological enterprise—the semiotic construction of a mythical Black community—renders the issue of generic taxonomy mute. What we have in the Morrison narrative is a situation somewhat similar to Boris Eichenbaum's description of Gogol's narrative strategy. Fredric Jameson restates Eichenbaum's position as follows: "Boris Eichenbaum is able to adjourn permanently the vexing problem of whether Gogol is to be considered a 'romantic' (the grotesques, the ghost at the end, the occasional pathos in tone) or a 'realist' (the evocation of Saint Petersburg, of poverty, of the lives of little people). For Gogol's starting point is not a 'vision of life,' not a meaning, but rather a style, a particular type of sentence he wishes to transpose to the level of the art-story, the gestures and storytelling techniques characteristic of the traditional Russian *skaz* or oral yarn. . . . It is because Gogol wishes to work in a particular kind of form and to speak in the tone of voice of the *skaz*, that

he casts about for raw materials appropriate to it, for anecdotes, names, piquant details, sudden shifts in manner." See Jameson, "Metacommentary," 114–115. My reading of Morrison is that the ideological commitment to the construction of a text that is racially specific might be viewed in a similar light. The fusion of numerous semiotic practices is dictated by textual enterprise; the representation of Black culture.

9. Toni Morrison, *The Bluest Eye* (New York: Washington Square Press, 1970), 34. Hereafter cited in the text by page number.

10. See Belsey, *Critical Practice*, 90–91.

11. Ibid., 70.

12. See M. M. Bakhtin, "Discourse in the Novel," in *The Dialogic Imagination: Four Essays by M. M. Bakhtin*, ed. Michael Holquist and trans. Caryl Emerson and Michael Holquist (Austin: University of Texas Press, 1981), 344–345.

13. See Fredric Jameson, *The Political Unconscious: Narrative as a Socially Symbolic Act* (Ithaca: Cornell University Press, 1982). Particularly illuminating is Jameson's discussion of the sea as a "privileged place" in Conrad's fiction (pp. 210ff.). Jameson argues that the sea is "both a strategy of containment and a place of real business: it is a border and a decorative limit, but it is also a highway, out of the world and in it at once, the repression of work . . . as well as the absence of the work-place itself."

14. The generalized description of the Black college in the novel is consistent with similar descriptions in Ralph Ellison's *Invisible Man* and Alice Walker's *Meridian*. Each writer argues that the college, through its attempt to "uplift" Blacks, contribute to their alienation and self-negation.

15. Linda Hutcheon, *A Theory of Parody: The Teachings of Twentieth-Century Art Forms* (London: Methuen, 1985), 53.

16. Toni Morrison, *Sula* (New York: New American Library, 1973), 4–5. Hereafter cited in the text by page number.

CHAPTER FOUR

1. See for example, Mary Helen Washington, ed., *Black-Eyed Susans: Classic Stories By and About Black Women* (New York:

Doubleday Anchor, 1975); and Dexter Fisher, ed., *The Third Woman: Minority Woman Writers of the United States* (Boston: Houghton Mifflin, 1980).

2. Critical treatment of the Afro-American short story is extremely limited. The only book-length manuscript that focuses on the subject is Robert Bone's *Down Home: A History of Afro-American Short Fiction from Its Beginning to the End of the Harlem Renaissance* (1975).

3. See "The Storyteller: Reflections on the Works of Nikolai Leskov," in Walter Benjamin, *Illuminations*, ed. Hazel Arendt (New York: Schocken Books, 1969), 87.

4. Toni Cade Bambara in an interview with Claudia Tate, in Tate, *Black Women Writers*, 25.

5. The construct inner world/outer world is adapted from Lotman's topological model of the literary text. Ann Shukman describes the model as follows: "The inner/outer opposition may be variously interpreted in different cultures and different texts as 'own people/other people,' 'believers/heathens,' 'culture/barbarity.' . . . The inner world/outer world opposition may also be interpreted as 'this world/the other world.'" One can see in Bambara's works two inscriptions that parallel this construct: the Black world/white world and the enclosed Black community/larger world oppositions. See Shukman, *Literature and Semiotics*, 95–96.

6. Werner Sollors, *Beyond Ethnicity: Consent and Descent in American Culture* (New York: Oxford University Press, 1986), 249–250.

7. Toni Cade Bambara, *Gorilla, My Love* (New York: Random House, 1972), 17. Hereafter cited in the text by page number.

8. For an interesting and illuminating study of body semiotics in Afro-American communities, see Benjamin G. Cooke's "Nonverbal Communication Among Afro-Americans: An Initial Classification," in *Rappin' and Stylin' Out: Communication in Black Urban America*, ed. Thomas Kochman (Urbana: University of Illinois Press, 1977), 32–64.

9. See William Riggan, *Picaros, Madmen, Naifs, and Clowns: The Unreliable First Person Narrator* (Norman: University of Oklahoma Press, 1981), 18.

10. Two Afro-American women scholars have produced significant research on these cultural practices. Grace Sims Holt, whose origins are southern and whose father was a minister, provides an insight into the ritual practices of the Black church and particularly the intense exchanges between minister and congregation. Claudia Mitchell-Kernan does an illustrated ethnographic reading of the linguistic culture of Blacks with particular emphasis on the practice of signifying. See Grace Sims Holt, "Stylin' Outta the Black Pulpit," and Claudia Mitchell-Kernan, "Signifying, Loud-Talking, and Marking," both in Kochman, *Rappin' and Stylin' Out*, 189–204 and 315–335.

11. Richard Wright uses this strategy throughout most of his fictional works, viewing "signifying rituals," as suggested in "Blueprint," as one of the dominant cultural traits of cultural nationalism.

12. See Laurent Jenny, "The Strategy of Form," in *French Literary Theory Today: A Reader*, ed. Tzvetan Todorov and trans. R. Carter (Cambridge: Cambridge University Press, 1982), 59.

13. I see in the treatment of sexual molestation in Bambara's work an interesting parallel to the manner in which Barthes discusses the representation of castration as the unnameable in Balzac's *Sarrasine*. See Roland Barthes, *S/Z: An Essay*, trans. Richard Midler (New York: Hill and Wang, 1974).

14. See Gloria I. Joseph, "Black Mothers and Daughters: Their Roles and Functions in American Society," in *Common Differences: Conflicts in Black and White Feminist Perspectives*, ed. Gloria I. Joseph and Jill Lewis (New York: Doubleday Anchor, 1981), 76.

15. See Helene Cixous, "The Laugh of the Medusa," in *The Signs Reader: Women, Gender, and Scholarship* (Chicago: University of Chicago Press, 1983), 283.

16. Toni Cade Bambara, *The Seabirds Are Still Alive* (New York: Random House, 1977), 9. Hereafter cited in the text by page number.

17. See Umberto Eco, *The Role of the Reader: Explorations in the Semiotics of Texts* (Bloomington: Indiana University Press, 1979). esp. 20–22.

CHAPTER FIVE

1. Walker, *Search*, 250–251. Hereafter cited in the text as *Search* and followed by page number.

2. See Hayden White, *Metahistory: The Historical Imagination in Nineteenth Century Europe* (Baltimore: Johns Hopkins University Press, 1973); and idem, "The Value of Narrativity in the Representation of Reality," in *The Content of the Form: Narrative Discourse and Historical Representation* (Baltimore: Johns Hopkins University Press, 1987).

3. Hayden White, "The Fictions of Factual Representation," in *Tropics of Discourse: Essays in Cultural Criticism* (Baltimore: Johns Hopkins University Press, 1978), 122. Another essay in the same collection cogently addresses these issues; it is "The Historical Text as Literary Artifact," 81d–100.

4. Gayle Greene and Coppelia Kahn, eds., *Making a Difference: Feminist Literary Criticism* (London: Metheun, 1985), 12–13.

5. See Walker's interview with Claudia Tate in Tate, *Black Women Writers*, 176.

6. While I would cautiously embrace the concept of character advanced by Joel Weinsheimer, it seems to have some relevance here. Weinsheimer argues: "Under the aegis of semiotic criticism, characters lose their privilege, their central status, and their definition. . . . As segments of a closed text, characters at most are patterns of reccurrence, motifs which are continually recontextualized in other motifs. In semiotic criticism, characters dissolve." Cited in Shlomith Rimmon-Kenan, *Narrative Fiction: Contemporary Poetics* (London: Metheun, 1983), 32. It is arguable that "characters dissolve" in fictive discourse, but what may happen, as in the case of Grange Copeland, is that the character traits become so clearly linked with the larger discourse (e.g., Grange's dehumanization and the sharecropping system in general) that character becomes essentially a medium for illuminating the major issue and thereby primarily a textual strategy.

7. The terminology here is again borrowed from Genette. The heterodiegetic narrator is a nonparticipant in the story he or she tells; the homodiegetic narrator is present as a character in his

narrative. See Gerard Genette, *Narrative Discourse: An Essay in Method*, trans. Jane E. Lewin (Ithaca: Cornell University Press, 1980), 244–245.

8. Alice Walker, *The Third Life of Grange Copeland* (New York: Harcourt Brace Jovanovich, 1970), 9. Hereafter cited in the text by page number.

9. See Paul Hernadi, "Dual Perspective: Free Indirect Discourse and Related Techniques," *Comparative Literature* 24 (1972): 32–43. Dorrit Cohn's theorizing of a "psychonarration" in which the narrator appropriates the speech and the thought of the character of a fictive discourse also addresses this narrative strategy. See Dorrit Cohn, *Transparent Minds: Narrative Modes for Presenting Consciousness in Fiction* (Princeton: Princeton University Press, 1978), 11. While it is not my intention to explore the debate related to this narrative strategy, my primary interest is its relationship to the production of textual ideology. What I am arguing is that in *The Third Life of Grange Copeland*, substitutionary narration or psychonarration results in a suppression of the histories of women.

10. Alice Walker, *Meridian* (New York: Washington Square Press, 1976), 117. Hereafter cited in the text by page number.

11. Jürgen Habermas, "Modernity Versus Postmodernity," *New German Critique*, no. 22 (Winter 1981): 5.

12. For an interesting reading of this narrative as one of several that focus on the issues of women's language and representational status, see Margaret Homans, " 'Her Very Own Howl': The Ambiguities of Representation in Recent Women's Fiction," *Signs: Journal of Women in Culture and Society* 9, no. 2 (Winter 1983): 186–205.

13. I am working here with the description of defamiliarization advanced by the Russian formalist Victor Shlovsky: "Habitualization devours works, clothes, furniture, one's wife, and the fear of war. If the whole complex lives of many people go on unconsciously, then such lives are as if they had never been. And art exists that one may recover the sensation of life; it exists to make one feel things, to make the stone *stony*. The purpose of art is to impart the sensation of things as they are perceived and not as they are known. The technique of art is to make objects

'unfamiliar,' to make forms difficult, to increase the difficulty and length of perception because the process of perception is an aesthetic end in itself and must be prolonged." See Victor Shlovsky, "Art as Technique," in *Russian Formalist Criticism: Four Essays*, ed. and trans. Lee T. Lemon and Marion J. Reis (Lincoln: University of Nebraska Press, 1965), 12. I have appropriated and modified this description of defamiliarization to argue that the unusual narrative strategies and frames Walker employs to represent motherhood place it as the site of oppression of women and force the reader to experience it in a different manner than he or she is accustomed to doing.

14. See, for example, "Advancing Luna—and Ida B. Wells," in Alice Walker, *You Can't Keep A Good Woman Down* (New York: Harcourt Brace Jovanovich, 1981), 85–104. In this narrative, the alleged rape of Luna by Freddie Pye provides the context for an extensive discussion of the responsibility of Black women to their race in general and to women as a class. It explores the terrors historically inflicted on Black men as the result of false accusations of rape and at the same time acknowledges that such acts sometimes occurred and were advocated by some extremists in the nationalist movements of the 1960s. The text assumes an interrogative modality, leaving the conclusion to the reader.

CHAPTER SIX

1. Eco, *Role of the Reader*, 63.

2. See Fredric Jameson, "Postmodernism, or The Cultural Logic of Late Capitalism," *New Left Review*, no. 164 (July–August 1984): 53–92.

3. Jean-Francois Lyotard, *The Postmodern Condition: A Report on Knowledge*, trans. Geoff Bennington and Brian Massumi (Minneapolis: University of Minnesota Press, 1984), 81.

4. Toni Morrison, *Tar Baby* (New York: Signet, 1981), 95. Hereafter cited in the text by page number.

5. Mikhail Bakhtin, *Problems of Dostoevsky's Poetics*, ed. and trans. Caryl Emerson (Minneapolis: University of Minnesota Press, 1984), 6. Katerina Clark and Michael Holquist further elabo-

rate on this concept by arguing that "the phenomenon that Bakhtin calls 'polyphony' is simply another name for dialogism. As Bakhtin admits: 'Every thought of Dostoevsky's heroes . . . senses itself to be from the very beginning a *rejoinder* in an unfinalized dialogue. Such thought is not impelled toward a well-rounded, finalized, systematically monologic whole. It lives a tense life on the borders of someone else's thought, someone else's consciousness'" (italics added by Clark and Holquist). See Katerina Clark and Michael Holquist, *Mikhail Bakhtin* (Cambridge: Harvard University Press, 1984), 242.

6. Alice Walker, *The Color Purple* (New York: Washington Square Press, 1982), 12. Hereafter cited in the text by page number.

7. M. M. Bakhtin, "Forms of Time and of the Chronotope in the Novel," in *The Dialogic Imagination*, ed. Michael Holquist and trans. Caryl Emerson and Michael Holquist (Austin: University of Texas Press, 1981), 123.

8. While the argument is developed in only a limited manner in the novel, "black" as it is used here is the sign of the undesirable. The reference is to intraracial prejudice, or what Walker labels "colorism," in which Afro-Americans of lighter complexion discriminate against the darker members of their race.

9. In a recent article in which Walker responded to the controversy created by the book, particularly its use of colloquial language and its construction of representations that some readers found offensive, she argues for the need to empower women such as Celie to use their own language to tell their stories. Equally important, she argues that rape and other forms of sexual exploitation should be placed within a discourse that is "shocking" so that their true nature is revealed. See Alice Walker, "Finding Celie's Voice," *Ms.*, December 1985, 71–72 and 96.

10. In her second collection of short stories, Walker uses even more graphic images to defamiliarize pornography. See particularly the stories "Porn" and "Coming Apart" in *You Can't Keep a Good Woman Down* (New York: Harcourt Brace Jovanovich 1971).

11. Sondra O'Neale offers a different reading and interpretation of the exploration of lesbianism in *The Color Purple*. In a highly provocative essay in which she generally criticizes Black women writers for failing to represent "black heroines" and for not ad-

dressing "those strengths that have made the black woman's survival possible," O'Neale argues that lesbianism is but one of several "avenues of escape" (others are mysticism, insanity, suicide, and religion) that can be viewed as solutions to the social and cultural problems confronting Black women. Within this context, she sees Celie's "choos[ing] lesbianism because no one who touches her life . . . will give her the attention, tenderness, and respect with which white and mulatto characters are showered." O'Neale's argument, it seems to me, strips Celie of free choice (it does not allow for the direct and sincere manner in which the novel depicts Celie to Shug) and dismisses the ideological significance of the representation of the lesbian relationship between the two women. See Sondra O'Neale, "Inhibiting Midwives, Usurping Creators: The Struggling Emergence of Black Women in American Fiction," in *Feminist Studies/Critical Studies*, ed. Teresa de Lauretis (Bloomington: Indiana University Press, 1986), 139–156.

12. If one accepts Greimas and Courtes's position (see A. J. Greimas and J. Courtes, *Semiotics and Language: An Analytical Dictionary*, trans. Larry Crist et al. [Bloomington: Indiana University Press, 1982], 238) that once a lexeme is written in an utterance, it becomes disambiguated, the widespread argument that "purple" functions in the novel as the sign of the gay and lesbian certainly has merit. Nevertheless, Walker's statement that "womanist is to feminist as purple is to lavender," seems to permit multiple meanings to be decoded. Purple can be the sign of womanist ideology in general or the specific evocation of lesbian ideology.

13. The conditions that Walker represents in Nettie's letters are central to the concerns of Black African feminists. Awa Thiam, who addresses the issue of the oppression of the Black woman in Africa, writes: "First of all, we must get rid of the myth that African societies are matriarchal. If people think that having a say in deciding on who the children should marry, organizing the domestic chores, and looking after the household is the same as having power, they are seriously mistaken. It is similarly a mistake to equate a matrilinear society to a matriarchal society. A woman's sole right is to have no rights.

"She has no real power, only a pseudo-power. She can act, insofar as she causes no embarrassment to her husband. She can exist, insofar as she does not upset the capitalist system. Thus, any power she may think she possesses is an illusion. The big decisions are the monopoly of the man, and she is not in any way involved in them. In Black Africa the Black man controls not only his own life, but also that of his wife." See Awa Thiam, *Black Sisters, Speak Out: Feminism and Oppression in Black Africa* (London: Pluto Press, 1986), 15; originally published by Editions Denoel, Paris, as *La Parole aux Negresses*, 1978.

14. Gloria T. Hull, "What I Think She's Doing Anyhow: A Reading of Toni Cade Bambara's *The Salt Eaters*," in *Home Girls: A Black Feminist Anthology*, ed. Barbara Smith (New York: Kitchen Table, Women of Color Press, 1983), 124.

15. Ibid., 137.

16. One might consider Benveniste's convincing discussion of semiotic systems, however, in which he posits an argument for nonredundancy: "The first principle [governing the relationships between semiotic systems] can be stated as the *principle of nonredundancy*. Semiotic systems are not 'synonymous'; we are not able to say 'the same thing' with spoken words that we can with music, as they are systems with different bases.

"In other words, two semiotic systems of different types cannot be mutually interchangeable. . . . [S]peech and music have as a common trait the production of sounds and the fact that they appeal to hearing; but this relationship does not prevail, in view of the difference in nature between their respective units and their types of operation. . . .

"Nonredundancy in the universe of sign systems occurs as a result of the nonconvertibility of systems with different bases. Man does not have several distinct systems at his disposal for the *same* signifying relationship." See Emile Benveniste, "The Semiology of Language," in *Semiotics: An Introductory Anthology*, ed. Robert E. Innis (Bloomington: Indiana University, 1985), 235.

17. Eleanor W. Traylor, "Music as Theme: The Jazz Mode in the Works of Toni Cade Bambara," in Evans, *Black Women Writers*, 65.

18. Ruth Elizabeth Burks, "From Baptism to Resurrection: Toni Cade Bambara and the Incongruity of Language," in Evans, *Black Women Writers*, 55–56.

19. Ibid., 56.

20. See Toni Cade Bambara, "What It Is I'm Doing Anyhow," in *The Writer on Her Work*, ed. Janet Sternberg (New York: Norton, 1980), 165.

21. Toni Cade Bambara, *The Salt Eaters* (New York: Random House, 1981), 64. Hereafter cited in the text by page number.

22. Jameson, "Postmodernism," 119.

23. Bakhtin, "Discourse in the Novel," 368.

24. See, for example, Mary Daly's discussion of the oppositional relationship of women's culture to patriarchy in *Gyn/Ecology: The Metaethics of Radical Feminism* (Boston: Beacon Press, 1978). For a general summary of radical feminist cultural practices as oppositional strategies and cultural and political interventions, see "Radical Feminism and Human Nature," in Alison M. Jaggar, *Feminist Politics and Human Nature* (Sussex, England: Rowman and Allanheld, 1983), 83–122.

25. The nationalist ideology of the text is evident in the exclusion of white women from this proposed united front. As in Bambara's earlier works, white females are marginalized by the politics of the work.

26. Bambara has commented on the representational status of the Seven Sisters, suggesting that they might become models for social action. See the interviews in the Tate and Evans works cited herein and the foreword to Cherrie Moraga and Gloria Andaluza, *This Bridge Called My Back: Writings by Radical Women of Color* (Watertown, Mass.: Persephone Press, 1981).

27. Jacques Derrida, *Positions*, trans. Alan Bass (Chicago: University of Chicago Press, 1972), 69–70. For a discussion of the relevance of Derrida's argument to postmodern textual practices in general, see Linda Hutcheon, "Beginning to Theorize Postmodernism," *Textual Practice* 1, no. 1 (Spring 1987): 10–31.

28. Williams, *Marxism and Literature*, 131.

29. Hortense J. Spillers, "Cross-Currents, Discontinuities: Black Women's Fiction," in *Conjuring: Black Women, Fiction, and Literary Tradition*, ed. Marjorie Pryse and Hortense J. Spillers (Bloomington: Indiana University Press, 1985), 251.

Bibliography

◆

Althusser, Louis. *Lenin and Philosophy and Other Essays*, translated by Ben Brewster. New York: Monthly Review Press, 1971.

Babcock, Barbara A., ed. *The Reversible World: Symbolic Inversion in Art and Society*. Ithaca: Cornell University Press, 1978.

Baker, Houston A., Jr. *Blues, Ideology, and Afro-American Literature: A Vernacular Theory*. Chicago: University of Chicago Press, 1984.

Bakerman, Jane. "The Seams Can't Show: An Interview with Toni Morrison." *Black American Literature Forum* 12 (1979): 56–60.

Bakhtin, M. M. *The Dialogic Imagination: Four Essays by M. M. Bakhtin*, translated by Caryl Emerson and Michael Holquist. Austin: University of Texas Press, 1981.

———. *The Problem of Dostoevsky's Poetics*, translated by Caryl Emerson. Minneapolis: University of Minnesota Press, 1984.

Bakhtin, M. M., and P. M. Medvedev. *The Formal Method in Literary Scholarship: A Critical Introduction to Sociological Poetics*, translated by Albert J. Wherle. Cambridge: Harvard University Press, 1985.

Bambara, Toni Cade. *The Black Woman: An Anthology*. New York: Signet, 1970.

———. *Gorilla, My Love*. New York: Random House, 1972.

———. *The Seabirds Are Still Alive*. New York: Random House, 1977.

———. "What It Is I'm Doing Anyhow." In *The Writer on Her Work*, edited by Janet Sternberg, 153–168. New York: Norton, 1980.

———. *The Salt Eaters*. New York: Random House, 1981.

———. "Salvation Is the Issue." In *Black Women Writers (1950–1980): A Critical Evaluation*, edited by Mari Evans, 41–47. Garden City, N.Y.: Doubleday Anchor, 1984.

Barbour, Floyd B., ed. *The Black Power Revolt: A Collection of Essays.* Boston: Porter Sargent, 1968.

Barthes, Roland. *Mythologies*, translated by Annette Lavers. New York: Hill and Wang, 1972.

———. *S/Z: An Essay*, translated by Richard Midler. New York: Hill and Wang, 1974.

Belsey, Catherine. *Critical Practice.* London: Methuen, 1980.

Benjamin, Walter. *Illuminations*, edited by Hazel Arendt. New York: Schocken Books, 1969.

Bernstein, Basil. "Social Class, Language, and Socialisation." In *Power and Ideology in Education*, edited by Jerome Karabel and A. H. Halsey. New York: Oxford University Press, 1977.

Braverman, Jane S. "Failures of Love: Female Initiation in the Novels of Toni Morrison." *American Literature* 52, no. 4 (1981): 541–563.

Brooks, Peter. *Reading for the Plot: Design and Intention in Literature.* New York: Vintage, 1985.

Bullins, Ed. "A Short Statement on Street Theatre." *Drama Review* 12 (Summer 1968): 93.

Burks, Ruth Elizabeth. "From Baptism to Resurrection: Toni Cade Bambara and the Incongruity of Language." In *Black Women Writers (1950–1980): A Critical Evaluation*, edited by Mari Evans, 48–57. Garden City, N.Y.: Doubleday Anchor, 1984.

Carby, Hazel V. *Reconstructing Womanhood: The Emergence of the Afro-American Woman Novelist.* New York: Oxford University Press, 1987.

Christian, Barbara. *Black Women Novelist: The Development of a Tradition.* Westport, Conn.: Greenwood Press, 1980.

———. *Black Feminist Criticism: Perspectives on Black Women Writers.* New York: Pergamon, 1985.

Clark, Katerina, and Michael Holquist. *Mikhail Bakhtin.* Cambridge: Harvard University Press, 1984.

Cohn, Dorrit. *Transparent Minds: Narrative Modes for Presenting Consciousness in Fiction.* Princeton: Princeton University Press, 1976.

Davis, Cynthia A. "Self, Society, and Myth in Toni Morrison's Fiction." *Contemporary Literature* 23, no. 3 (1973): 323–340.

de Lauretis, Teresa, ed. *Feminist Studies/Critical Studies*. Bloomington: Indiana University Press, 1986.

Derrida, Jacques. *Positions*, translated by Alan Bass. Chicago: University of Chicago Press, 1981.

De Weever, Jacqueline. "The Inverted World of Toni Morrison's *The Bluest Eye* and *Sula*." *College Language Association Journal* 22, no. 4 (June 1979): 402–414.

Eagleton, Terry. *Criticism and Ideology: A Study in Marxist Literary Theory*. London: Verso Press, 1982.

Eco, Umberto. *The Role of the Reader: Explorations in the Semiotics of Texts*. Bloomington: Indiana University Press, 1977.

Eisenstein, Zillah R., ed. *Capitalist Patriarchy and the Case for Socialist Feminism*. New York: Monthly Review Press, 1979.

Evans, Mari, ed. *Black Women Writers (1950–1980): A Critical Evaluation*. Garden City, N.Y.: Doubleday Anchor, 1984.

Fabre, Michel. *The Unfinished Quest of Richard Wright*, translated by Isabel Barzun. New York: Morrow, 1973.

Fisher, Dexter, ed. *The Third Woman: Minority Women Writers of the United States*. Boston: Houghton Mifflin, 1980.

Foucault, Michel. "Nietzsche, Geneaology, History," in *Language, Counter-Memory, Practice: Selected Essays and Interviews by Michel Foucault*, translated by Donald Bouchard and Sherry Simon, 139–164. Ithaca: Cornell University Press, 1977.

———. *Power/Knowledge: Selected Interviews and Other Writings 1972–1977*, edited and translated by Colin Gordon et al. New York: Pantheon, 1980.

Fuller, Hoyt W. "Towards a Black Aesthetic." In *The Black Aesthetic*, edited by Addison Gayle, Jr., 3–11. New York: Doubleday Anchor, 1972.

Gayle, Addison, Jr., ed. *The Black Aesthetic*. New York: Doubleday Anchor, 1972.

Geertz, Clifford. *Local Knowledge: Further Essays in Interpretive Anthropology*. New York: Basic Books, 1983.

Gennette, Gerard. *Narrative Discourse: An Essay in Method*, translated by Jane E. Lewin. Ithaca: Cornell University Press, 1980.

Giddings, Paula. *When and Where I Enter: The Impact of Black Women on Race and Sex in America*. New York: Bantam, 1985.

Gilbert, Sandra, and Susan Gubar. *The Madwoman in the Attic: The Woman Writer and the Nineteenth-Century Imagination.* New Haven: Yale University Press, 1979.

Goldmann, Lucien. *Towards A Sociology of the Novel,* translated by Alan Sheridan. London: Tavistock, 1978.

Gordon, Linda. "What's New in Women's History." In *Feminist Studies/Critical Studies,* edited by Teresa de Lauretis, 20–30. Bloomington: Indiana University Press, 1986.

Greenblatt, Stephen. *Renaissance Self-Fashioning: From More to Shakespeare.* Chicago: University of Chicago Press, 1980.

Greene, Gayle, and Coppelia Kahn, eds. *Making a Difference: Feminist Literary Criticism.* London: Methuen, 1985.

Greimas, A. J., and J. Courtes. *Semiotics and Language: An Analytical Dictionary,* translated by Larry Crist et al. Bloomington: Indiana University Press, 1982.

Habermas, Jürgen. "Modernity versus Postmodernity." *New German Critique,* no. 22 (Winter 1981): 3–15.

Hamilton, Charles. "Riots, Revolts, and Relevant Responses." In *The Black Power Revolt: A Collection of Essays,* edited by Floyd B. Barbour, 171–178. Boston: Porter Sargent, 1968.

Harding, Vincent. "Black Power and the American Christ." In *The Black Power Revolt: A Collection of Essays,* edited by Floyd B. Barbour, 85–93. Boston: Porter Sargent, 1968.

Hemenway, Robert. *Zora Neale Hurston: A Literary Biography.* Urbana: University of Illinois Press, 1977.

Hernadi, Paul. "Dual Perspective: Free Indirect Discourse and Related Techniques." *Comparative Literature* 24 (1972): 32–43.

Homans, Margaret. " 'Her Very Own Howl': The Ambiguities of Representation in Recent Women's Fiction." *Signs: Journal of Women in Culture and Society* 9, no. 2 (Winter 1983): 186–205.

Hovet, Grace Ann, and Barbara Lounsberry. "Flying as Symbol in *The Bluest Eye, Sula,* and *Song of Solomon.*" *College Language Association Journal* 27, no. 2 (December 1983): 119–140.

Hurston, Zora Neale. *Mules and Men.* New York: Harper & Row, 1970.

––––––. *Their Eyes Were Watching God.* Urbana: University of Illinois Press, 1978.

Hutcheon, Linda. *A Theory of Parody: The Teachings of Twentieth-Century Art Forms*. London: Methuen, 1985.

———. "Beginning to Theorize Postmodernism." *Textual Practice* 1, no. 1 (Spring 1987): 10–31.

Innis, Robert E., ed. *Semiotics: An Introductory Anthology*. Bloomington: University of Indiana Press, 1985.

Jaggar, Alison M. *Feminist Politics and Human Nature*. Sussex, England: Rowman and Allanheld, 1983.

Jakobson, Roman. "The Dominant." In *Readings in Russian Poetics*, ed. Ladislav Matejka and Krystna Pomorska, 82–87. Cambridge: MIT Press, 1971.

Jameson, Fredric. *The Political Unconscious: Narrative as a Socially Symbolic Act*. Ithaca: Cornell University Press, 1982.

———. "Postmodernism and Consumer Society." In *The Anti-Aesthetic: Essays on Postmodern Culture*, edited by Hal Foster, 111–125. Port Townsend, Wash.: Bay Press, 1983.

———. "Postmodernism, or the Cultural Logic of Late Capitalism." *New Left Review*, no. 164 (July–August 1984): 53–92.

———. "Metacommentary." In *Contemporary Literary Criticism: Modernism Through Post-Structuralism*, edited by Robert Con Davis, 111–123. New York: Longman, 1986.

Jenny, Laurent. "The Strategy of Form." In *French Literary Theory Today*, edited by Tzvetan Todorov and translated by R. Carter, 34–63. Cambridge: Cambridge University Press, 1982.

Johnson, Barbara. "Thresholds of Difference: Structures of Address in Zora Neale Hurston." *Critical Inquiry* 12, no. 1 (Autumn 1985): 278–289.

Jones, LeRoi, and Larry Neal, eds. *Black Fire*. New York: Morrow, 1968.

Joseph, Gloria I., and Jill Lewis. *Common Differences: Conflicts in Black and White Feminist Perspectives*. New York: Doubleday Anchor, 1981.

Karenga, Maulana Ron. "The Quotable Karenga." In *The Black Power Revolt: A Collection of Essays*, edited by Floyd B. Barbour, 162–170. Boston: Porter Sargent, 1968.

———. "Black Cultural Nationalism." In *The Black Aesthetic*, edited by Addison Gayle, Jr., 31–37. New York: Doubleday Anchor, 1972.

Kavanagh, James H. "To the Same Defect: Toward a Critique of the Ideology of the Aesthetic." *Bucknell Review* 29, no. 1 (1972): 102–123.

Kochman, Thomas, ed. *Rappin' and Stylin' Out: Communications in Black Urban America*. Urbana: University of Illinois Press, 1977.

Kristeva, Julia. *Desire in Language: A Semiotic Approach to Literature and Art*, edited by Leon S. Roudiez and translated by Thomas Gora, Alice Jardine, and Leon S. Roudiez. New York: Columbia University Press, 1980.

Kuhn, Annette. *Women's Pictures: Feminism and Cinema*. London: Routledge and Kegan Paul, 1982.

Lacan, Jacques. *Speech and Language in Psychoanalysis*, translated by Anthony Wilden. Baltimore: Johns Hopkins University Press, 1981.

LaCapra, Dominick. *Rethinking Intellectual History: Texts, Contexts, Language*. Ithaca: Cornell University Press, 1983.

Lane, Bonnie Shipman. "Toni Morrison's Rainbow Code." *Critique: Studies in Modern Fiction* 24, no. 3 (Spring 1983): 173–181.

LeClair, Thomas. "A Conversation with Toni Morrison: 'The Language Must Not Sweat.'" *New Republic* 184 (March 21, 1981): 25–29.

Lee, Dorothy H. "The Quest for Self: Triumph and Failure in the Works of Toni Morrison." In *Black Women Writers (1950–1980): A Critical Evaluation*, edited by Mari Evans, 346–360. Garden City, N.Y.: Doubleday Anchor, 1984.

Lyotard, Jean-Francois. *The Postmodern Condition: A Report on Knowledge*, translated by Geoff Bennington and Brian Massumi. Minneapolis: University of Minnesota Press, 1984.

Marable, Manning. *How Capitalism Underdeveloped Black America: Problems in Race, Political Economy, and Society*. Boston: South End Press, 1983, 69–103.

McKay, Nellie. "An Interview with Toni Morrison." *Contemporary Literature* 24, no. 4 (Winter 1983): 413–429.

Morrison, Toni. *The Bluest Eye*. New York: Washington Square Press, 1970.

———. *Sula*. New York: New American Library, 1973.

———. *Tar Baby*. New York: Signet Press, 1981.

———. "Rootedness: The Ancestor as Foundation." In *Black Women Writers (1950–1980): A Critical Examination*, edited by Mari Evans, 339–345. Garden City, N.Y.: Doubleday Anchor, 1984.

Neal, Larry. "The Black Arts Movement." *Drama Review* 12 (Summer 1968): 29–39.

O'Neale, Sondra. "Inhibiting Midwifes, Usurping Creators: The Struggling Emergence of Black Women in American Fiction." In *Feminist Studies/Critical Studies*, edited by Teresa de Lauretis, 139–156. Bloomington: Indiana University Press, 1986.

Pouissant, Alvin F. "The Negro: His Self Image and Integration." In *The Black Power Revolt: A Collection of Essays*, edited by Floyd B. Barbour, 94–102. Boston: Porter Sargent, 1968.

Rimmon-Kenan, Shlomith. *Narrative Fiction: Contemporary Poetics*. London: Methuen, 1983.

Robinson, William, ed. *Nommo: An Anthology of Modern Black African and Black American Literature*. New York: Macmillan, 1972.

Shlovsky, Victor. "Art as Technique." In *Russian Formalist Criticism: Four Essays*, translated and edited by Lee T. Limon and Marion J. Reis, 3–24. Nebraska: University of Nebraska Press, 1965.

Shukman, Ann. *Literature and Semiotics: A Study of the Writings of Yu. M. Lotman*. Amsterdam: North Holland, 1977.

Smith, Barbara, ed. *Home Girls: A Black Feminist Anthology*. New York: Kitchen Table, Women of Color Press, 1983.

Sollors, Werner. *Beyond Ethnicity: Consent and Descent in American Culture*. New York: Oxford University Press, 1986.

Spillers, Hortense J. "Cross-Currents, Discontinuities: Black Women's Fiction." In *Conjuring: Black Women, Fiction, and Literary Tradition*, edited by Marjorie Pryse and Hortense J. Spillers, 249–261. Bloomington: Indiana University Press, 1985.

Stepto, Robert. "Intimate Things in Place: A Conversation with Toni Morrison." In *Chant of Saints: A Gathering of Afro-American Literature, Art, and Scholarship*, edited by Micheal S. Harper and Robert B. Stepto, 213–229. Urbana: University of Illinois Press, 1979.

Tate, Claudia, ed. *Black Women Writers at Work*. New York: Continuum, 1983.

Thiam, Awa. *Black Sisters, Speak Out: Feminism and Oppression in Black Africa*. London: Pluto Press, 1986.

Todorov, Tzvetan. *The Poetics of Prose*, translated by Richard Howard. Ithaca: Cornell University Press, 1977.

Traylor, Eleanor W. "Music as Theme: The Jazz Mode in the Works of Toni Cade Bambara." In *Black Women Writers (1950–1980): A Critical Evaluation*, edited by Mari Evans, 58–70. Garden City, N.Y.: Doubleday Anchor, 1984.

Turner, Darwin T. "Theme, Characterization, and Style in the Works of Toni Morrison." In *Black Women Writers (1950–1980): A Critical Evaluation*, edited by Mari Evans, 361–369. Garden City, N.Y.: Doubleday Anchor, 1984.

Voloshinov, V. N. [M. M. Bakhtin?]. *Marxism and the Philosophy of Language*, translated by Ladislav Matejka and I. R. Titunik. New York: Seminar Press, 1973.

Walker, Alice. *The Third Life of Grange Copeland*. New York: Harcourt Brace Jovanovitch, 1970.

———. *Meridian*. New York: Washington Square Press, 1976.

———. *You Can't Keep a Good Woman Down*. New York: Harcourt Brace Jovanovich, 1981.

———. *The Color Purple*. New York: Washington Square Press, 1982.

———. *In Search of Our Mothers' Gardens: Womanist Prose*. New York: Harcourt Brace Jovanovitch, 1983.

———. "Finding Celie's Voice." *Ms.*, December 1985, 71ff.

Washington, Mary Helen. *Black-Eyed Susans: Classic Stories by and about Black Women*. New York: Doubleday Anchor, 1975.

White, Hayden. *Tropics of Discourse: Essays in Cultural Criticism*. Baltimore: Johns Hopkins University Press, 1978.

———. *The Content of the Form: Narrative Discourse and Historical Representation*. Baltimore: Johns Hopkins University Press, 1987.

Williams, Raymond. *Keywords: A Vocabulary of Culture and Society*. Oxford: Oxford University Press, 1976.

————. *Marxism and Literature*. Oxford: Oxford University Press, 1977.

————. *Problems in Materialism and Culture*. London: Verso Press, 1980.

Winner, Irene Portis. "Ethnicity, Modernity, and the Theory of Culture Texts." In *Semiotics of Culture*, ed. Irene Portis Winner and Jean Umiker-Sebeok, 103–147. The Hague: Mouton, 1979.

Wright, Richard. *White Man, Listen*. New York: Doubleday Anchor, 1964.

————. "Blueprint for Negro Literature." In *Richard Wright Reader*, edited by Ellen Wright and Michel Fabre, 36–49. New York: Harper & Row, 1978.

Wynter, Sylvia. "Sambos and Minstrels." *Social Text* I (1979): 149–156.

Index

◆

Black, 32–34, 100, 105; sexual
exploitation of, 46–53, 66, 76,
78–81, 100–102, 136–137, 148,
167

Wright, Richard, 24–26, 29, 42,
44, 57, 91, 194n. 20, 202n. 11
Writing, differences in Black and
white women's, 8–9